FROM THE
REARVIEW
MIRROR

FROM THE
REARVIEW
MIRROR

Reflections of a Culver
Academies' Instructor

JOSEPH M. HORVATH

Archway Publishing books may be ordered through booksellers or by contacting:

Archway Publishing
1663 Liberty Drive
Bloomington, IN 47403
www.archwaypublishing.com
844-669-3957

ISBN: 978-1-6657-1726-7 (sc)
ISBN: 978-1-6657-1727-4 (hc)
ISBN: 978-1-6657-1728-1 (e)

Library of Congress Control Number: 2022905012

Print information available on the last page.

Archway Publishing rev. date: 3/17/2022

Contents

I dedicate this work to my Hungarian American parents, Joseph and Margaret Horvath, who referred to their fifth son as their "schoolteacher" son. One rarely hears the term "schoolteacher" today, but they were as proud of me as they were all my siblings. To their credit, they recognized well that their fifth offspring did not possess a mechanical bone in his body and would need to make his way in this world with advanced studies in an academic arena. That domain eventually proved to be in the realm of education, and I am grateful and relieved that my parents' wisdom led me to such a path in life.

Preface

Thirty-four years spent at Culver have allowed for a myriad of reflections from the "rearview." Although deserving of inclusion in these snapshots of memories, I recognize that countless names and characters have been omitted. I assure that those very people also have played pivotal roles in my own development as a member of the Academies. I regret not having recorded notes contemporaneously of episodes that caused me to ponder, warmed my heart, and touched my soul. Please note, however, that my reflections of Culver could not have been as detailed or as colorful without those experiences. I wish to thank every student I engaged in and out of the classroom, every graduate who became a part of Culver's alumni, every parent who sacrificed by relinquishing sons and daughters to attend this august institution, and every faculty and staff member whom I valued as a colleague and friend. Upon this "rearview mirror" reflection, I have concluded that these were the best years of my life.

The Culver Song

'Round Aubeenaubee Bay, the leaves were falling softly,
When one September day, I saw those towers lofty.
I heard the bugle call, and took my place at Culver.
I'll find no honor greater than to be a Culver grad.
Back, back to Culver days, the song my heart sings ever,
No matter where I roam, 'tis Culver, Culver, Culver.
To hear the bugle call … old memories how they thrill me,
And proud am I of Culver, and to be a Culver grad.

"Packy"

First Glance

September 1983 was my second year at Culver after a first in which I continually questioned whether I belonged at this boarding-prep-military-private school. I struggled mightily throughout my first year with finding my own niche, much like Culver was also doing. The fact that the school had several different names underscored this identity crisis. Most of the faculty and staff appeared firmly entrenched in this unique way of life that simultaneously appealed to and confounded me. The school laid claim to being a "family," but I had not yet embraced this notion.

The first day of classes this year found me teaching a section of American history (more precisely nineteenth- and twentieth-century American history) during the first period, quite early in the morning. I discovered rather soon that Culver names and acronyms meant more to the established veterans of this community than they would to me. The syllabus for the nineteenth-century American history class actually began with a unit on the Constitutional Convention in the late eighteenth century. The dean of the Academies explained that the state of Indiana gave our students credit for government if we taught our American history classes to include a background into the events of 1787 in Philadelphia. This appeared strange, but the exemption status remained intact for over a decade during my teaching tenure. As the students sauntered into the antiquated yet cozy classroom in the basement of the Memorial Library (the History Department was housed in a series of catacombs, resembling ancient Rome), I noticed one young man who took his place in the last seat of the second row. The class sizes were maximized at twenty, so camouflaging oneself into the background was nearly impossible. I also observed that he arrived at class with no notebook, no textbook, and no pen or pencil. Throughout the usual awkwardness of any first day in class, he appeared disinterested, aloof to any information I was providing about the course. Class on the second day replicated much like the first. He carried with him no study materials whatsoever. I detained him briefly when class concluded and suggested that he come better prepared on day three. To my chagrin, my words had fallen on deafened ears, and Patrick had reached the point when my patience yielded to impatience. Vicariously learning about America's past simply would not be acceptable. By the end of the first week, Patrick possessed study materials, but he lacked focus. His half-opened eyes betrayed him every step of the way. Perhaps I thought that he simply did not get enough sleep, because this class did meet early in the morning each day. Perhaps I thought he was patently disinterested and bored. I am not certain to what extent I leaned one way or the other. I do know that I decided that this kid was not going to get the upper hand, and with every opportunity, I tried to bore a hole through that impervious facade of his.

Soon into the first marking period, I made contact with his counselor. Patrick, a member of the Troop organization, did not have a particularly warm relationship with the counselor. I suspect that Patrick did not have a close relationship with most of the adults in his life. I learned much about Patrick in that telephone conversation. Prior to Culver, Patrick's life had been both traumatic and tragic. Several years earlier, fire had badly damaged his family home in the western suburbs of Cleveland, Ohio. The conflagration had killed his mother and youngest brother and severely burned his eldest brother. Patrick had escaped relatively unscathed physically, but the emotional and psychological scars readily were apparent. Upon learning of these circumstances, I decided then and there that

Patrick would be my number one project for the year. Perhaps this speaks as much about me as anything else. I needed to fit in at Culver; I needed to become a part of that Culver family about which people spoke. Maybe this was what was meant by "in loco parentis," which I kept reading in our school literature. I learned a bit more about the young man who occupied the last seat in the second row. Patrick's father had remarried. His new wife was a pert understudy actress on Broadway, and unquestionably, she was never to occupy the place in Patrick's life that he had reserved for his own mother. Patrick referenced his family as the three remaining older brothers, his father, and finally, and a bit grudgingly, his stepmother.

Private Lessons

Not only was I Patrick's history instructor, but I also took up the challenge of tutoring him in English and mathematics. Writing, grammar, and literature posed no problems for me. Geometry and trigonometry were another story. I found myself asking mathematics instructors to teach me so that I in turn could tutor my protégé. This was no small feat, I assure you. I had believed that as long as one could balance one's checkbook, one would have no need for higher levels of mathematics. Addition, subtraction, multiplication, and division would get me by in this world. When it came to the Pythagorean theorem, well, let's just say that the reason is most discernible why courses in the humanities and languages rather than mathematics and sciences drew my attention.

Gradually, Patrick came more frequently and voluntarily to my humble apartment in Main Barracks for assistance. As we prepared for the upcoming fall parents' weekend, I had a brilliant idea of how to get Patrick's father "off his back," as Patrick stated. Coincidentally, I believed that this would illustrate that Culver was a good place for Patrick to grow academically and socially. I coached Patrick in many of the questions and answers that would be discussed for the Friday parents' day lesson. Let's be completely candid here. I fed Patrick both the questions and the responses. All he would be required to do was to engage himself in the conversation, which he rarely would do on any given day. To suggest that Patrick was taciturn in class would be akin to intimating that Culver has a hockey program. Unscrupulous? Yes. Dishonest? Absolutely. Lacking integrity? Unquestionably. For a good cause? Well, one can judge for oneself. I was convinced that I needed to win over Patrick so that he would realize that I was not merely his teacher but his friend, someone whom he could trust.

Parents weekend came, and I met Patrick's father and stepmother. I liked them immediately. Actually, I liked them a great deal. Somehow Patrick's description of them did not resonate with what I observed. After some introductory comments from me, I began rapidly to fire questions at the class, posing as a would-be Socrates confronting his student Plato. With each question, I looked pleadingly toward Patrick. Why was he not raising his hand and impressing his father? It must have been halfway through the class period that I noticed Patrick looking as if he might raise his hand. I pounced at the slightest opening he would provide. My star pupil did not disappoint. A few minutes later, and a second correct response to one of my inquiries was given. This time I gazed more directly at the father, rather than the student. His broad smile spoke volumes. Two questions and two correct answers! When the class concluded, Patrick's father rushed to my desk and embraced me as hard as anyone ever has. He was clearly ecstatic with his son. We talked a good while, and I am certain that I shortchanged the other students' parents because I have no recollection of speaking with any of the rest of them. Success! I convinced myself that this moment in time was worth the deception. Somehow, I think that Socrates would have disapproved. No matter. The private lessons shared with Patrick opened the door wider to our familial relationship.

I was now a part of the Culver family.

"Fine!"

During many of the private tutoring lessons, Patrick's responses vacillated between reluctant hesitancy and perfunctory compliance. When I suggested, implored, or demanded measured steps to prepare for serious academic pursuits, he inevitably gritted his teeth and uttered, "Fine!" At one moment the "fine" echoed a tone of sarcasm; at another, it carried a measure of resignation. It was as if he simply wanted the lesson to end and for me to set him free. Inevitably, whenever the two of us were not on the same page, in the same book, in the same library (as I used to relate to him), "fine" popped up out of nowhere and became the most overused word in our lexicon. Occasionally, I resorted to writing "fine" on top of his papers just to mock him in much the same manner as he would torment me. To this day, this word cannot be spoken or written without Patrick dominating my thoughts.

Driving between the Cones

Spring brought warmer weather and a relocation of our lessons: outdoors. This time, instead of history, English, or geometry punctuating our conversations, we got behind the wheel of my 1980 Ford Mustang and began driving lessons. More accurately, they would be described as parking lessons. One of the outcomes of the house fire was that Patrick's eyes had been damaged. He had little depth perception, and his peripheral vision had become impaired. We spent many an afternoon on asphalt at Woodcraft Camp, attempting to park between bright orange cones that I had commandeered from campus security. I wrongly had assumed that parking my compact Mustang would be less challenging for Patrick. My hope was to instill some self-confidence so that he would be able to secure his driver's license when he returned home to Ohio for the summer. We kept these lessons to ourselves because I anticipated that Patrick would not want others to know of his "parking deficiencies." Most teens are excited and anxious to obtain their drivers' licenses when they attain the legal age to do so. But Patrick displayed no desire whatsoever. I understood far better than he thought I could. I too had struggled with my own driver's education when I was a teen. I knew all too well how embarrassing this could be for a teen. Suffice it to say, Patrick encountered many frustrations with these sorts of lessons.

The patience for both of us was put to the most severe test. However, in the process, we evolved into a twosome, more than teacher and student. We joked. We laughed. We poked fun at ourselves and each other. We spoke of goals in life. We discovered that we had more in common than we had ever imagined. Oh, yes, we listened to music.

Bonding Patrick and me as friends seemed rather absurd, but music played a pivotal role in precisely accomplishing that. Throughout our many conversations, I learned that Patrick preferred the music of my era to that of his. Surprisingly, he was well versed with the lyrics from some of my favorites: the Everly Brothers, Ricky Nelson, and Simon and Garfunkel among them. Neither of us possessed any sort of musical talent on our own, but we both recognized good music, music that sang to our souls. I remember one such occasion when I informed him that he had been born a generation too late. He quickly retorted that I may have been as well. At the time, I did not realize that he was poking me about being out of touch with the world around me. Only later would I come to appreciate his acerbic wit. He was a lad after my own heart!

That summer I purchased the greatest hits collection of Simon and Garfunkel on vinyl records and mailed them to Patrick for his birthday on July 15. I was certain that he would smile when he opened his gift from his history instructor at Culver. I also wondered if he had passed his Ohio driver's exam. I would later learn that he did not.

Senior Year at Long Last

Patrick became a senior during 1984–85, and although I did not instruct him formally in a classroom setting, we remained teacher and pupil via tutoring lessons. The curriculum this year, however, broadened to include trips to the Dairy Queen, shopping mall, pizza parlor, and movie theater. One film, surely not a classic in my estimation, *Fast Times at Ridgemont High,* evoked utter laughter from both of us, undoubtedly for far different reasons. For Patrick, the mockery by students of their teacher struck a familiar chord. For me, the absurdity of attempting to explain the geopolitical world of the 1980s to malcontents in a public-school environment seemed preposterous. Humor has a way of solidifying bonds.

In late autumn, I moved out of my barracks apartment into an ultramodern Swiss chalet home several blocks from campus. I had not seen Patrick for over a week, and I did not have a chance to tell him of my move since the opportunity to relocate happened suddenly. After a second week elapsed, I received a telephone call from Patrick's father. He explained that his son had come to my barracks apartment several times, and I did not answer the door. I was surprised that he had not attempted to find me in my classroom in the History Department, but upon second thought, I should not have been surprised by anything Patrick did or did not do. Rather than waiting for Mohammed to come to the proverbial mountain, I merely set out the next night to locate Patrick in his North Barracks quarters. Making my way up the staircase and down the newly polished corridor (our custodial staff on campus was first rate), I flung open Patrick's door and observed him listening to Simon and Garfunkel's *"Sounds of Silence."* He said, "Where have you been, Mr. Horvath? I have been searching for you forever." In my mind I questioned, but did not verbalize, how diligent he had been in his quest to track me down. I doubted seriously that he would ever make it as a sleuth. Nevertheless, the two of us reconnected after a two-week hiatus from one another.

The crisp days of autumn yielded to the Midwestern winds of December. As it happened, I was assigned a chaperone bus to Cleveland for the holiday break. Patrick and I, along with roughly forty or fifty other Culver students, traveled the nearly six-hour excursion by motor coach. Patrick's father and stepmother invited me to stay with them overnight before I returned to Indiana and then on to Michigan to spend Christmas with my own family. I accepted the invitation, largely because I wanted to witness firsthand the family dynamics but also because I liked this family. They were no-nonsense people. They were pragmatic, straightforward, and unpretentious, and I greatly appreciated their candor. I don't recall anything out of the ordinary about my visit, other than the fact that Patrick was very uncomfortable. It may have been attributable to my presence, or perhaps he simply felt out of his comfort zone. His "home" turf resembled more a foreign terrain, as much for him as it was for me.

The rest of the winter and into the spring progressed much like all Culver winters and springs. The eventual destination was graduation and processing through the gate for the cadets and the arch for the coeds. All Culver first classmen and seniors are fixated on these events. When graduation weekend arrived, all three of Patrick's brothers came to support their youngest sibling. So too did his grandparents (his mother's parents), his father, and his stepmother. We held a party for Patrick at the home that I was renting, and for the first time in two years, I witnessed a broad smile on the face of our graduate. His happiness infected us all. Raucous laughter, hearty embraces, joyous tears, and excessive pride dominated the scenes for the entire weekend. Particularly impressive was the Lancer performance in which Patrick, along with his fellow troopers, performed acrobatic stunts on their horses. When they escorted their steeds into Lake Maxinkuckee following their final show, Patrick was a sight of sore eyes. His family acknowledged him as he took center stage, and he reveled in all of their attention.

As the weekend came to a halt, the pit in my stomach enlarged to such an extent that I felt quite ill. The signal was unmistakably clear to me; my time with Patrick at Culver was rapidly concluding. The gnawing feeling of having to say goodbye to my protégé lurked on the horizon. As a graduation gift I gave Patrick an engraved pewter mug with a gun-shaped handle. The inscription was "Packy, make sure that you always aim straight in life." I finally referred to him by his preferred name of Packy. For two years I had resisted, if for no other reason, than to ensure that I retained the upper hand in our relationship. I knew that everyone else referred to him as Packy, and I wanted to preserve that my relationship with him was distinctive from all the others. Besides, I knew that it would irk him whenever I called him Patrick! When Packy departed with his family for Ohio, I pondered when our paths might, if ever, cross again. I hugged him and told him that I would be in touch with him quite often. His response was simply "Fine."

College and Beyond

Packy enrolled at Ohio University in Athens, Ohio, in the fall of 1985. I struggled a bit in my role at Culver in his absence. It seemed oddly different to me to walk the majestic campus and realize that he was hundreds of miles away. Dozens of new faces awaited my attention, but I honestly do not recall any of them needing me as I thought that Packy did. I do know that I channeled most of my energies into coaching in our boys basketball program that year, but something was missing; emptiness dominated my existence.

Occasionally, I did hear from Packy during his frosh year in college, usually in the form of lengthy letters. He remarked more than once that he rejoiced in the freedom that he experienced in Athens. The constraints that he felt at Culver dissipated, and he now relished the chance to sleep late in the morning, attend or not attend a class lecture, or socialize with college mates well into the evening and early morning hours. He also related that his campus mates looked at him oddly when he referred to going to the "mess hall" to eat his meals. In short, he became the proverbial freshman at college, transitioning from adolescence to adulthood with all of the usual missteps along the way.

Packy's sophomore year in Athens did not progress as I thought it would, and our communication with one another waned. I did send Christmas greetings, and when his birthday arrived in July, I did similarly. Since I did not hear from him in some time, I telephoned his father to learn about my "wayward student." I discovered that Packy was now in Texas. I do not remember why he was there, except perhaps a girlfriend or another friend had enticed him to come to the Lone Star State. The very next day I received a chilling phone call from Patrick's father. We had just spoken the prior day, and he wanted to share with me some horrible news. Texas law enforcement authorities had informed him that Packy had died sometime during the night. My blood ran cold on that hot, sultry July day of 1987. I want to think that I endeavored to comfort Packy's father the best that I possibly could over the telephone. A father had just informed me that he lost his son. Years earlier he lost his youngest son in addition to his wife in a devastating fire. I want to think that I understood the gravity of the tragedy that hovered over this fellow. I doubt that I could have grasped the full extent or depths of his loss. The truth probably rests more closely with me dealing with my own loss. My protégé, Packy, was gone; he was really gone. When I hung up the telephone receiver, I lay on my bed and wept into my pillow. An integral part of me died with that ill-fated telephone call.

The events surrounding the funeral near Cleveland were simply overwhelming. I was not prepared for what I was to experience in the coming days. I stood outside in a line that extended for more than a block to get into the funeral home for the visitation. July's excessive heat and humidity caused me as much discomfort as the trepidation of approaching the interior of the funeral home. Packy's father came outside for a break and noticed that I was standing amid the awaiting crowd of mourners. He retrieved me from the line, and we embraced. It was the same sort of embrace that he displayed when he came for a Culver parents weekend several years earlier. He insisted that I take a place near the family and the greeting line. He held one of my arms, and Packy's stepmother held the other as I made my way to the open casket. I found myself leaning back; this is a natural tendency, or so I am told, under such circumstances. There lay Packy, rosary in hands, with longer hair and puffier cheeks than I had remembered when he was seventeen and we were parking my Mustang between the orange cones at Woodcraft Camp. I told myself, "This isn't Packy." I also recall thinking of his nickname Packy and not Patrick.

I knelt at his coffin and said a few prayers as I closed my eyes resolutely, hoping that the enveloping tears would not be visible to the others at the visitation. That is what I did for the rest of my time in Ohio: I shut my eyes to the world around me. I ended up staying in Packy's bedroom for the night before the funeral Mass the next day. I noticed the pewter mug that I had gifted him for graduation on top of his wardrobe dresser. I did not sleep the entire night. Suffice it to say, emotions took center stage for one and all of us. The church, the cemetery, and the reception at the house exhausted every ounce of energy that I could muster. All I wanted to do was to leave Ohio and return to Culver. When an opportune time arose for me to depart, I hugged and kissed Packy's father and stepmother and told them that we would remain in close contact. My return trip home included an extra parcel; Packy's stepmother returned the pewter mug I had given him in June 1985. My eyes were transfixed by the inscription, "Packy, make sure you always aim straight in life." The endless ride from Cleveland to Culver gave me ample opportunity to reflect. One thought kept haunting me over and over. *Packy took his own life. Packy took his own life. Packy took ...*

Never, Ever Again

I walked along the edge of the Lake Maxinkuckee shoreline late one summer night in 1988. The brightness of the moon illuminated my steps along the cracked sidewalk that outlined the periphery of the campus. A cool wind caressingly blew across the cascading waves reaching the northern extremity of the lake. How many times I solitarily had walked this path! Infrequently, I did so with neighbors and friends. These moments were reserved for quiet reflections about relationships, about work, about aspirations, about life. I loved these sojourns because they afforded me an opportunity to think with no one interrupting my thoughts. On this particular night, the most idyllic of all summer nights, I was at peace with myself and the world around me. The moon, glittering on the lake, was particularly intense. As I leisurely followed the sidewalk toward North Barracks, a silhouette image ricocheted from one of the windows. I slowed the pace as I became mesmerized by what I was viewing. Standing adroitly and facing the window in question, I recognized the familiarity of this site. This was the window to Packy's room in the barracks when he was a senior. Memories, both distant and recent, momentarily crashed my placid world. I peered at my watch. It was 12:01 a.m., July 15, 1988, Packy's birthday.

When I glanced again at Packy's window, the moon's reflection had vanished, and all I could recognize was the blackness of night. I vowed, "Never, ever again." I never wanted to invest so much of myself in another student who profoundly might impact me as Packy had. It was a promise that I repeatedly broke during my Culver career.

God bless you, Packy. I miss you, and I really am "fine."

Packy and I reviewing an exam together

Postcards, Retreats, Greenies, and Clio's House

A Fascination with Postcards

Approaching spring break during my first year at Culver, I learned that the two-plus weeks afforded all of us time to travel great distances far and wide. In fact, I decided to spend one week in Colorado, visiting a dear aunt of mine, and the second week along the Gulf Coast of Florida, spending time with my brother and his family. Many students' impatience became quite visible as the calendar made its way to late March and early April. Most were jetting to their global destinations, and I proposed that they could gain some extra credit if they sent me a postcard from their vacation spots. Since I had quite a fascination with postcards and in fact collected them over the many years of my own travels, I thought these new additions would supplement my own card assemblage.

Upon returning from spring break, I visited the post office to collect more than two weeks of mail, including more than forty postcards from the seventy-odd number of students I was instructing. Undoubtedly, we have become familiar with the phrase "pretty as a postcard," and this aptly described the variety that I received. I recall such locales as New York City's

Central Park, Orlando's Disney World, Seattle's Space Needle, the Rocky Mountain ski country of Aspen, Colorado, the Alamo in San Antonio, Texas, and other domestic locations. International arrivals from Mexico, Canada (ever from the hockey contingent), Jamaica, and Saudi Arabia complemented those from the states. One postcard, however, captured my attention as much, if not more than, any of the others. This one was from the beaches of Florida, depicting "naked buns" lying in the sand on the front of the postcard. Reading the transcription on the reverse side was a simple "Having a great time, Mr. Horvath. Glad that you are not here!" It was signed, "The Buns." I even queried the post office personnel if they chuckled or perhaps guffawed when placing the card in my mailbox. I should add that the carefully printed message was camouflaged in such a manner that I would be unable to detect the sender. Quite naturally, I asked all of the students in my classes, "Who was the mystery writer?" I would not be able to give any extra credit to an anonymous source. Alas, no one came forward to claim ownership of said postcard. I secretly laughed and came to realize that this was a rather innocent prank on the instructor and thought better not to display it, with the other postcards, on the classroom bulletin board since the spring parents' weekend would soon occur in May.

During my second year at Culver, I found that I again made the same request of students prior to exiting for spring break. Extra credit also would be the reward for mailing me a postcard. Once again dozens of students sent their postcard greetings from many parts of the globe. This particular year seemed to have a more international flavor as more students set their sights abroad. Clearly, they were a globetrotting group. Retrieving this batch of arrival cards provided just as much anticipation as the first year because I remembered students telling me of their travel plans. "Déjà vu, all over again," as one of the cards was "naked buns on the beach," this time from Acapulco, Mexico. The reverse side again, neatly printed, revealed, "Having a great time, Mr. Horvath. Glad that you are not here!" Signed, "The Buns." As was the case during the first year, the authorship of this card remained unidentifiable. I believed that the same person or persons sent both of these "naked buns" cards because the printing and the message were precisely the same.

The third year, and then the fourth, and then the fifth and so on for a total of seventeen years, this story repeated itself over and over and over again. Each year, the message on the card was exactly the same, but scenes of a sandy beach in Greece, Hawaii, Costa Rica, Philippines, California, Texas, or France added to the variety of the collection itself. Every year, not a single claimant to one of these, which again reinforced my notion that they all were written by the same source. The sleuth in me thought that during alumni weekends I might sniff out a few details from classmates. No such luck whatsoever! The hijinks lived on for seventeen years, and I tipped my hat to the prankster.

For whatever reason, I stopped requesting postcards from students. I am uncertain as to why or even when I did so. However, I recollect telling this story to one of my advanced placement government and politics classes, and one rather enterprising student offered his reason as to why the seventeen-year cycle ended the way that it did. This student, not being the least bit comical or crude, suggested three possible reasons for the termination of "beach buns" postcards: one, the former student may have died; two, the former student is now married, and the spouse said that this foolishness should stop; three, the former student no longer "gives a damn about you, Mr. Horvath." I chose to believe it was either option one or option two.

Retreat, but Not of the Culver Variety

John Mars, Culver's tenth superintendent, retired in 1982 just as I was making my entrance into the Academies. I regretted that I was not able to work under his administrative leadership because of the empathy, intellect, and devotion to service he exhibited. Nonetheless, he and I established a friendship bond, largely established upon our Roman Catholic roots. Dean Mars introduced me to the works of Thomas Merton, an American theologian and scholar of comparative religion. Merton was born in France in 1915 and eventually settled in the United States. He was received as a novice by the Abbey of Gethsemani, a monastery in Kentucky in 1941, and tragically died in Bangkok,

Thailand, in 1968. Merton's influence, while residing at this monastery, proved to be preeminent among theologians of many denominations. Dean Mars informed me that he long had wished to spend a week retreat at Gethsemani, but for a multitude of reasons (probably the rigors of his many jobs at Culver), he was unable to complete the retreat. He suggested that I embark upon such a religious excursion to this Trappist monastery, and so I did in the summer of 1993. That week in June proved to be one of the most spiritually uplifting ones in my life.

Upon arrival at Gethsemani in Trappist, Kentucky, I was greeted by one of the monks who explained how the Monday through Friday schedule would operate. This particular retreat would be one that was considered self-guided. In other words, visitors (who were limited to thirty per week) could engage in as many of the services and activities as they wished. This Trappist monastery was based upon the Cistercians of France, and the work of the monks revolved around prayer, sacred reading, and work. Silence was preserved to foster a climate of prayer although speaking was permitted in designated areas only. In fact, signs everywhere indicated, "Silence is the only language spoken here!" I decided that I would go full throttle and adhere to the vow of silence during my retreat. Seven different prayer services, beginning at 3:15 a.m. and concluding at 7:30 p.m., were offered by the monks. I also elected to attend each of these seven on the days I visited. Between these prayer times, those of us on retreat could engage in the work conducted by the monks, such as making cheese, peanut brittle, jelly, honey, and coffee.

Never having been on a silent retreat before, I was rather apprehensive about approaching the weekly schedule. My eyes and ears were open to new vistas, new sensations, and new prayers. I noticed a balding, short, fortysomething monk on the first day and determined then and there that I would follow his every move. In large part, I made this selection based upon the fact that we appeared to be contemporaries; many of the other forty-plus monks were vintage octogenarians. When this fellow was tasked with preparing breakfast, so would I. When he labored in the dairy section of the 2,000-acre Kentucky hilltops making cheese, I followed suit. I found shadowing him in the vineyards a bit taxing in the summer sun, but I kept thinking of the grapes transformed into merlots or cabernets. The intense June heat seemed more tolerable when I allowed myself to think of wine. Maybe it was prayer-like thoughts, but in retrospect, I doubt many prayers silently were recited at these times.

The daily seven-prayer services, sometimes accompanied with chants, sometimes in restful silence, provided alternate versions and styles to my accustomed manner of praying. As the regimen of very early rising became more routine, I discovered that the stillness permeating the Abbey at Gethsemani allowed for contemplative reflection. "Good for the soul," I reminded myself. I would not suggest that I had incurred a midlife crisis, but my spiritual batteries required recharging. I thought about John Mars and how much he would have profited from ambling along those same paths that Thomas Merton once trekked. As each service concluded, one by one, the monks promenaded from the main level of the church below the balcony where the visitors on retreat knelt and prayed. I was struck by the devout nature of each monk, but I was particularly attentive to my "partner" whenever I viewed him from the lofty perch of the balcony. In my prayers, I asked God to help me become more pious in my daily life; perhaps He could help me become even more monk-like.

The retreat's conclusion was at the noon service on Friday, and I became somewhat melancholy. I realized that I never had the opportunity to express to my "partner monk" that shadowing him appeared somewhat life-altering. Here is where the silence became deafening because it seemed important that I convey gratitude for allowing me to be a part of this monastic life, a part of this monk's life. I never received a single gaze, much less an affirmation from this fellow for the entire retreat. As the promenading monks exited the church, I noticed that "my monk" was the last in line. Kneeling at the window glass that separated the balcony from the rest of the church interior, I closed my eyes and thanked God that I experienced the life at Gethsemani. When I peered at the recessing monks, the last in the procession glanced up at the balcony (most assuredly at me, I thought), nodded his head one time, and withdrew from sight. One brief glance, one slight nod, and one brisk departure—never before did the sound of silence (with all deference to Simon and Garfunkel) resonate so lyrically with me.

Military Mentors behind the Scenes

If ever there existed a group of individuals more underappreciated on campus, I would suggest that the military mentors for CMA would be that group. When I first heard the term "greenie," I was a bit confounded. Clearly, the cadets were not referring to my beloved Spartans from East Lansing, Michigan. Instead, this was the "affectionate" or perhaps "disrespectful" term for those who daily guided and supported the various units in their military responsibilities. Certainly, the names of commandants were more recognizable to the rest of campus. From Carl Steely to Bob Meek, Mike Wockenfuss, Al Shine, Mike Kehoe, Kelly Jordan, and Mike Neller, most of the armed services were represented within the hierarchy of CMA administration. Undoubtedly, they deserved such recognition because of their status position and laborious efforts to infuse principles of leadership within the corps of cadets. That said, I believe it lay in the hands of these greenies to perform the daily mentoring of the young men of Culver. As such, I found these men worthy of the highest praise that Culver Military Academy afforded.

The day of moving into my Main Barracks apartment arrived, and Lt. Dale Smith not only greeted me but helped me move my belongings into the "palatial" abode on the second floor of Main Barracks. I realized immediately why Dean Nagy had not shown me my lodgings when I interviewed for the position earlier that summer. Let's just say that the "spartan" digs were not my idea of "Spartan" (Michigan State green and white) hospitality. Nevertheless, I was quite taken with Lt. Smith's cordial welcoming, and I felt a sense of calm since the military aspect of Culver had caused some trepidation for me. I believe that Dale Smith only remained for my first year, but whenever we saw each other, he inevitably inquired as to my acclimation to my new environs. (I think he referred to something more than the two-room faculty apartment.)

During that first year, I encountered Chip Thorpe, a second classman in the Band, from Marysville, Ohio. Chip, a gregarious fellow, had not yet passed his boards, and this was rather unusual for someone who was in his third year at Culver. I learned that he was frightfully apprehensive about the entire process, so I offered to assist him in his preparation. In that process, I learned a bit about a cadet's indoctrination to Culver history and military leadership. Suffice it to say, Chip eventually did pass his boards, and we developed a mutual fondness for one another. He later asked if I would chaperone the trip to his hometown in Ohio where the Grenadiers (precision rifle and drill team) would perform in a parade. This entailed a weekend excursion away from Culver, and together with S.Sgt. Robert Williams, the Grenadiers' mentor, I witnessed firsthand the results of laborious preparation that these young men and their mentor had exerted.

Stepping out of my classroom and into an unfamiliar world, I returned to Culver quite impressed. This experience prompted me to observe other military groups with more zeal, particularly if I discovered that a number of these cadets were students in my classes. Lancer platoons, four-gun drills, rangers, and the honor guards were just some of the notable military ensembles that over the years I watched with greater appreciation for their pride and precision. Of course, special occasions, such as the Veteran's Day Ceremony, the Memorial Day Gold Star Ceremony, and Presidential Inaugural Parades, showcased the military component of CMA in its most dramatic ways. Camera footage of these events is replete with the beauty and reverence of such performances.

As rich and colorful as special CMA events could demonstrate, the greenies who served as military mentors to each of the company units (infantry, battery, cavalry, and band) accomplished far more than merely assisting the counselor in charge of an organization. Trucks, canons, rifles, swords, horses, and musical instruments all needed coordination and oftentimes instruction. Who best would provide this backdrop to Sunday and retreat parades, room and clothing/hair inspections, nightly study conditions as barrack inspectors, officers in charge of campus conditions, coaching athletic and extracurricular teams, and so many miscellaneous items that popped up at a moment's notice? The greenies, of course. These men, each unique in demeanor, style, and background, deserve recognition because of their service to CMA and the entire school. In the humblest manner possible, I would salute all of those who filled these roles. I am especially proud to have known, laughed with, and learned from the likes of M.Sgt. James Smith, who served also with me in the History Department, M.Sgt. Mark Click, whose good-natured barbs entertained all around the dining hall breakfast table, CPO Todd Wallingford, my "deer hunting" companion, and CSM (R) Brett Rankert, my early morning workout partner at the fitness center. They, and many others, were and are the unsung heroes for their military service prior to Culver. Since green is my favorite color, these men became favorite cohorts of mine as well.

CSM (R) Brett Rankert with Collin Parker (CMA '13) at West Point graduation

Rooms and Occupants of Clio's House

My entrance into the world of Culver included becoming a member of the House of Clio, as the Department of History referred to itself. Clio, the muse of history in Greek mythology, undertook additional significance as the department members prided themselves in the study of antiquity through modernity. I recalled some in the department referencing the House of Clio possessing several rooms to include more than history. Namely, rooms of geography, philosophy, psychology, government and politics, and economics would find comfort and solace within the entire structure of history. Clio's arms were wide and welcoming. I joined this august group in 1982 as a full-time instructor with my fellow full-time cohorts, L. K. Moore (department chair), Robert B. D. Hartman, Richard Davies, David Sampson, and Eugene Twardosz. The part-time members included counselors who taught one course in addition to their residential life responsibilities. These members were Janet Stannard, Anthony Mayfield, William Roth, and Major George Runkle. Robert Meek, an academic dean, and Alexander Nagy, principal and dean of the Academies, completed the part-time membership. These six "interlopers," as I referred to them, brought the department total to twelve distinctive personalities.

What struck me most about that first year in the House of Clio was that each member took pride in the courses that were taught and the preparation exerted to stimulate interest in these disciplines. I won't suggest that I was overly intimidated by the longevity or pedigree of some of the members, but I do remember that I needed to step up my game for fear that I might be the neophyte hire who could not live up to the lofty expectations of Chairman L. K. Moore. Nearly half of those members of that original department have now passed on, but I still hold them in high regard because of their scholarship and service to Culver. Department "cookie nights," final examinations on black lapboards in Eppley Auditorium, and honors papers review boards may have passed their time, much as have the chalk, eraser, and blackboard. Eventually, the History Department merged with the English Department to form a new entity, namely the Humanities Department. Many arduous discussions and committee assignments labored before the two became one. The jury is still out whether this transformation strengthened the curriculum and increased student understanding of both history and English. In some cases, aligning the curricula of both at the grade levels made logical sense. (Teaching American history and American literature during the junior year was a positive realignment.) In others, it was akin to putting a square peg in a round hole. Perhaps this new animal was designed inherently to offer new insights, such as enhanced critical thinking and greater clarity of verbal expression. Members of both departments were tasked with examining the strengths, challenges, and goals for such a major overall.

In many ways, this period of flux precipitated considerable angst for many members of both departments. As chair of history, I too wrestled with such a metamorphosis. Was I being true to the historian in my soul? Was I becoming an impediment to growth? How was growth to be measured? Could it be measured? If so, how? In the end, I took solace in the fact that effective teaching and learning required both a solid command of and passion for the subject matter. These, combined with a love for one's students, would result in success, however that may be calculated. With the passage of time, some noted historians in this country bemoan the fact that history appears to be a lost discipline. I would reinforce this by reminding, "History is for all ages." If this truism is realized, then the rooms and occupants in the Clio's House would remain vibrant.

Clio's History Department in 1982-83
(Photo courtesy of The Culver Academies)

The Black-Clad Lad from the Bluegrass State

October 1984 brought me face-to-face with one of the most remarkable and unforgettable people in my life. Basketball practice had begun at the Academy, and I assisted the head coach for CMA. Opening weeks of tryouts revealed players of various skills, knowledge, and passion. Culver Military Academy did not possess a heritage of basketball success, not terribly surprising since "Hoosier hysteria" was embedded in nearly every Indiana school, no matter how small or large. CMA had participated in the Indiana High School Athletic Association for less than a decade. Needless to say, we were Johnny-come-lately on the basketball hardcourts. While watching the would-be players run, dribble, and shoot, I could not help but notice this one rather skinny, young man wearing black shorts. The black shorts, tightly gripping his narrow hips, distinguished him from the rest of the group who dressed in maroon attire, part of the school colors. He was a new second-classman (junior) at Culver, but the determination exerted by his demeanor caught my eye as much as did the black shorts. A few days into the tryout period, I noticed that the boy was absent from practice. Several more practices followed with more absences. I wondered why this seemingly driven fellow abandoned the basketball program. (I learned later that he had returned to Kentucky to attend the funeral of his grandmother). The next week the black-short clad boy reappeared. He approached me and inquired, "Did I miss anything, Coach, while I was gone?" I sarcastically replied that he had been cut from the program. My sense of humor (many have labeled it wicked) was lost entirely upon him. I can still visualize his utterly devastated countenance when I cavalierly informed him of his fate. He dejectedly turned from me, and I realized that I needed to run after him to suggest that I was merely jesting. His eyes lit like a July firecracker, and his infectious smile signaled that an endearing relationship between us would soon bloom. Bland Ballard Matthews from Shelbyville, Kentucky, did indeed make the varsity roster of Culver Military Academy, and no one was happier than I was. (Well, maybe Bland himself was!)

Bland Ballard had been an American Revolutionary War hero and statesman from Kentucky, and his parents' naming their youngest child after this man served noticed to family and friends that their pride in their son was befitting of historical lore. More about history will follow. Bland's first year at Culver (and my third) found that our paths crossed largely in the basketball arena and less within the academic quads on campus. His schedule that included elementary German did allow the two of us to engage one another with pithy German phrases, trying to increase our lexicon *auf Deutsch*. I would yell, "Ausgezeichnet!" ("Excellent!") when Bland would make a play on the court worthy of such praise. His teammates quizzically gazed at him and then me, shrugged their shoulders, and thought this undoubtedly was some sort of secret play being concocted.

We experienced a rather mediocre record during Bland's junior year. Actually, we had more talent than what our wins and losses would reveal, but a few of the players needed attitude adjustments, which hampered our ability to vanquish our opponents on the court. This became further evidence to me that Bland was a high-caliber young man. He remained positive and upbeat and sought criticism from all the coaches. I knew that this was also the case with his teachers without ever having to solicit information from them about this "bluegrass" player. Bland's parents paid a winter visit from Kentucky to Culver to watch him play a weekend basketball game, but as January in the Midwest can be, the snows, winds, and temps erupted into an old-fashioned storm, and the weekend games were canceled. Nonetheless, I became acquainted with Bill and Else Matthews and gained some insight into the Matthews family dynamic.

I knew that Bland had two older sisters, Lisa and Ellen, and one older brother, Beau, who graduated from Culver in 1975. Beau was quite the basketball star in his playing days at Culver, and I think that I began to see, in part, why Bland was so dedicated and passionate about improvement on the court. Although Bland never explained to me that he was competing with the legacy of Beau's exploits (Beau had some game-winning shots that even the dean of the Academy, Dean Nagy, would marvel over), I thought that he was trying to prove his basketball prowess as much to his older brother as he was to himself. The one initial memory of meeting Bill and Else was that they claimed that the relationship between Bland and me was evolving into one of a mutual admiration society with one another. I thought that was an apt description of our association with one another. It extended beyond coach/player to perhaps mentor/mentee.

When spring break arrived in late March, I drove Bland home to Shelbyville. The opportunity to witness firsthand the small hometown of the Matthews family and play some tennis in warmer weather also afforded me a chance to visit Else's antique store. Her entrepreneurial spirit surprised me a bit. I had not imagined that she was the consummate shopkeeper. Bill was absent during my visit, on business somewhere, as it was explained to me by the family. It would be some time later that I came to understand that Bill's absence was more normalcy than his presence. Perhaps Else's occupation with her own shop helped to explain how she independently maneuvered life. I did not meet Bland's siblings during this visit, but I wondered what they were like. I know that I came away from that spring visit not altogether certain what to think of Bland's family. I knew that I wanted to like them for Bland's sake, so I decided then and there that I would indeed like them. They were different in many regards to my own family, but I felt that religious or political differences should always take a back seat to values and ethics. Else's fierce independence could be overwhelming at first glance, but I began to appreciate her strength and forbearance for what it appeared to be: a coping mechanism in day-to-day living.

The remainder of the school year found that Bland and I enjoyed an occasional dinner in the dining hall together. We spoke often of his aspirations in life, college interests, and of course, basketball. I knew that he was a bright, talented young man in the classroom, as many of his instructors related to me. I also knew that Bland could enhance his academic record even more if he exerted a stronger effort in preparation for each course. In short, he coasted a bit because he thought he could. Perhaps his classes in public school in Kentucky did not challenge him as they should, and he felt that he could get by with a good effort rather than an outstanding one. I scolded him that if he ever found himself in my classroom, things might be a tad different. He nodded, but I could discern that he was not convinced. I was not about to allow this kid from the Bluegrass State to get the better of me in a classroom environment. I would learn a year later that Bland did get the better of me on more than one occasion. Reflectively, I can state unequivocally that I could not be prouder of this fact. Before Bland departed for the summer, he gave me a photo of himself, posing in basketball attire. The note that he wrote on the back of that photo touched me deeply. He penned the words that I should think about him, working assiduously on both his basketball and academic skills. He would do so because he wanted me to be proud of him and thanking me for having such confidence in him. I became teary-eyed whenever I read that notation, which I frequently did that summer and have occasionally since then when going through my personal artifacts. I missed that black-clad lad that summer of 1985 more than words can describe. I believe it was during this time that I began to think of him as my adopted son. I doubt that he needed an adopted father, but I know that he had filled an enormous void in my life. I could not have been more blessed.

In August 1985, Bland's senior year arrived. I eagerly awaited the return to campus of my Kentucky blue-blooded star. Bland returned to school a bit early in an attempt to make the CMA tennis team. Culver has always had a penchant for superlative tennis players enrolling in the school. Many of these players originated from Latin America, and they brought with them a certain flair for the flamboyance on the tennis courts. Bland found himself a bit overwhelmed by some of the stars of the team and succumbed to them in the team tryouts. Nonetheless, I think that he enjoyed the competitiveness of a sport that was not necessarily his forte.

The biggest news of the start of classes was that Bland was enrolled in my American history course. It was not the advanced placement section that he had hoped to select, but I developed a plan that would ensure he would not suffer from a lack of serious pursuit. In short, this was the appropriate time for me to turn up the heat in my classroom expectations. Remember I was not about to allow Bland to coast his way through any class of mine. I think this may have caused numerous students to drop the class throughout the semester, but I knew that this protégé of mine would never dare contemplate such action. At least I convinced myself that he would not.

During the second semester, as we approached the May advanced placement examination period, I made the request (Bland may recall this as more of an imperative than request) that he should visit my home on early Saturday mornings to prepare him for taking the AP exam in US history. He may not have had the benefit of taking the course, but I was determined that he would be prepared successfully to write an outstanding test. In hindsight I did not think much of the sacrifice he was making by relinquishing sleep on a Saturday morning. He certainly never complained about it to me prior to the exam. After the exam was completed, this became a different matter. Let the record show that Bland relished having his Saturday morning sleep-ins again. Let the record also indicate that when the scores were announced in July, Bland scored a five on the AP US history exam. He deserved all of the credit and acclamations afforded to him.

Aside from those private tutorial lessons in US history, Bland distinguished himself as a gentleman and a scholar within the class of 1986. He would garner cum laude status by the time graduation arrived;

however, he did not allow his social life to be diminished. Needless to say, Bland kept a keen eye out for the prettiest gals in the class, and unquestionably, many of them were dazzled by his southern charm. It was amazing to witness how this Kentucky bluegrass fellow developed a thicker drawl whenever he approached the girls. You would swear that the twang in his voice became just a bit more drawn in these social settings.

Nevertheless, basketball was still the driving force in Bland's life, and his senior season with CMA would eventually turn out to be an eventful one for him. He had improved considerably his skills as evidenced on the court. Most discernibly, his work during the summer between his junior and senior years paid dividends. The won-loss record may have remained in the mediocre category, but without some of the personality and attitude issues from the previous season, I think we were a more likable group with whom to work and compete. Bland's roommate, Tommy Mortell, became an ally for him on and off the court, and they have remained friends all their lives.

A new assistant coach arrived on the scene as well. Harry Frick, a rather colorful character, was a gifted and knowledgeable coach who stressed fundamentals more than other coaches Bland had encountered. Tip drills became the norm when players did not perform in practice. Players jokingly mocked Coach Frick behind his back, but to a player, I don't think any of them disrespected his coaching techniques and flair for wardrobe attire. Let's just say that Harry Frick needed no haberdasher to offer clothing advice. It appeared that he might spend more money on his clothing allowance than on his housing. I would suggest that two important cogs in Bland's wheelhouse for his senior year of basketball were both his roommate, Tommy, and Coach Frick. Both contributed mightily into Bland's development as a player and person.

I was fortunate enough to meet Bland's siblings during his senior year. On one winter weekend of basketball (this time without snow cancellations), Bland's father and sister arrived to watch him play. I liked Ellen quite a bit. She had a certain panache that was both charming and endearing. It was this particular weekend that my faculty intern, Patrick McHugh, an Eastern-bred liberal through and through, clashed with Ellen. They were contemporaries, but somehow that is all that they seemingly had in common. Initially, I thought that they were flirting with one another in a good-natured way. As the weekend wore on, it became obvious, even to the most obtuse fellow, that there was a dislike for one another. To this day, I do not understand why. I knew Patrick very well. He worked with me in the classroom for the entire year, and I liked and respected him much, and not merely because of his progressive orientation that I shared with him. I liked Ellen because of that sass, and besides, she was Bland's sister. Of course, I would like her. I even made the trek to Louisville for her wedding later in the fall of 1986. Sometimes, situations and people don't mesh as one might think that they should. Perhaps that is part of life's mysteries, not knowing the whys and wherefores that only the Lord can explain.

As the academic year was approaching commencement, I found myself becoming more and more subdued around Bland. I would be losing my "adopted" son to college in the fall, and like any parent, I assume, it was with mixed emotions that I would have to bid adieu. We had ventured together to visit both Purdue University and the University of Notre Dame on college visits. Secretly I had hoped that he would select Notre Dame because he would be closer to Culver and to me. I did not comprehend what his family wished for him, and for that I was deeply ashamed of myself. I think that my own self-interests took center stage. I told myself that I wanted the best for Bland, and to a certain degree, I still believe that I held his best interests in my heart. Maybe my interests were too dominant in the entire college acceptance process. At any rate, commencement weekend arrived, and with it came Bland's entire family. His parents and all of his siblings, Lisa, Beau, and Ellen, happily joined in the celebration. We all crowded together in my humble abode, and we enjoyed basking in Bland's accomplishments during his two-year stint at Culver. A highlight for me was witnessing Bland receiving the A. E. K. Cull Award for promise and talent in the field of history. All of those Saturday morning tutorial lessons paid off, did they not?

When the weekend concluded and Bland departed a couple of days afterward, I felt as if my job at Culver was completed only after three years. Saying goodbye to Patrick McHugh, who had taken a job at a Quaker school in Philadelphia, and then embracing Bland one last time left me emotionally drained. I may have even cried in my proverbial beer. Number 33, as he wore on his CMA basketball uniform, was now making his way in life without my eyes gazing over his shoulders. I thought again of our chance first encounter on the practice basketball courts and my cavalier dismissal of telling him he had been cut from the team. I was no longer that sharp-tongued coach attempting acerbic humor. I could find no humor in letting go of Bland. I would be reminded later in life by a close priest friend who said, "Letting go is the easy part of any relationship. It is the holding on that is so difficult."

Bland and I, bonded by basketball

The Black-Clad Lad from the Bluegrass State: The Sequel

Since Bland's graduation from Culver in 1986, I have had ample opportunities to remain connected with him, some on a frequent basis, others more sporadically. Before matriculation to the University of Notre Dame in the autumn of 1986, I visited Bland while he was working in the coal mines of eastern Kentucky. Irvine, Kentucky, appeared to be one of the most forsaken of Appalachian towns. I marveled at Bland's ability to navigate the blue-collar work he engaged while reading voraciously from great literary works. It was also during this summer visit that I returned to Shelbyville to see the Matthews household. The most memorable event was helping his sister Lisa mow their hilly yard. Somehow one of the unattended mowers plunged its way into the family swimming pool. Lisa's version of what occurred differed drastically from my account. Bland informed me that his family had the impression that it was I who was the culprit in the lawnmower/swimming pool accident. I was both bewildered and bothered by such a tale, but over time, this story has remained legendary in Matthews family folklore.

Bland's mother, Else, drove him from Kentucky to drop her youngest child for college at the University of Notre Dame. They stopped in Culver, and I accompanied them in helping Bland get situated in his new dormitory domicile. I was honored to be included in this exercise since Bill was unable to make the trek to South Bend. What struck me most of this weekend was the frank discussion that Else and I had about our lives after depositing Bland for his entrance into college. Else, who had always remained quite formal (and sometimes aloof) around me became emotional when speaking about her own life. Perhaps it was the thought of sending her final child off on his own. Perhaps it had more to do with her stage in life. Perhaps it was a combination of the two. Whatever the reason, I came to appreciate Else in a manner that I had not experienced previously. She seemed far more vulnerable, and this allowed for a stronger bond between the two of us. I believed that she appreciated my assistance in working with Bland for the past two years.

I learned from Bland much later that this period of time for the Matthews family was fraught with turmoil, and the decision to attend Notre Dame was not met with overwhelming endorsement by most of the Matthews family members. I thought it might have been the Roman Catholic connection that interfered with the lack of support. Needless to say, I was taken aback by this situation, and after two years of attending Notre Dame, Bland would make the decision to transfer to the University of Louisville. I was disappointed, but I also realized that I probably interfered far too much in Bland's college matriculation to Notre Dame and needed to take a step backward in his life. What was it that my priest friend told me? "Letting go is the easy part of any relationship. It is the holding on that is so difficult."

During Bland's two years at Notre Dame, I visited him for dinners, attending Catholic Mass with him and his girlfriend, Molly, at the Basilica of Sacred Heart, and occasionally taking him shopping. Bland called me frequently to inform how his progress was taking shape. His math and science classes, which were to prepare him for a career in engineering, were challenging to say the least. The one good aspect of these courses was that it proved that he was not cut out to be an engineer. Business was more to his liking. It would suit his personality and his spirit of entrepreneurship. I recall Bland also telling me that he was trying out for the men's basketball program, headed by Coach Digger Phelps. At the time, I chuckled because I knew that basketball, which was the origin of our connection, was still the link that the two of us could share. In the final analysis, Bland was unable to make the squad as a walk-on, but I applauded his tenacity in following through with his passion.

Once Bland departed Notre Dame, our communication and connections with one another suffered considerably. No one was to blame for this sort of occurrence. The busyness of life and raw emotions probably were attributable to our separation. I felt that I needed to allow Bland to fly solo, and I also believed that it was not in his best interests to listen to my opinions, which might have conflicted with his parents and siblings.

After several years of each of us going our own directions, Bland and I did renew our friendship. It happened during one of Culver's glorious May reunion weekends. Bland explained to me many things that he was experiencing, most of which I had been completely unaware. It was as if I may have been the most clueless person on the face of this earth. Here was my "adopted" son revealing matters that simultaneously opened my eyes and broke my heart. I was overcome with guilt in not being able to offer comfort and support when Bland might have needed it most. Busyness in life and raw emotions are not excuses for negligence in lending a helping hand. I reminded myself to read my favorite biblical scripture, which is Ecclesiastes 4:9–10.

> Two are better than one; because they have a good reward for their labour. For if they fall, the one will lift up his fellow; but woe to him that is alone when he falleth; for he hath not another to help him up.

To this day, I read this scripture at least once a week and contemplate if I am letting someone down without a helping hand to lift him up. Even as I pen these words to paper, I recognize that I fail to live these words more often than not. I don't want to appear as if I possess a martyr complex, but my Roman Catholic guilt brings me back to reality. I need to do better in this regard, putting others first before my own self-interests.

Bland and I continued to delve into each other's life, usually at Culver reunions but also when major events occurred that we wanted to share with one another. Bland's marriage to Marcie and the births and growths of his two sons, Nolan and Ian, clearly served as high benchmarks in his life to share with his former coach and teacher. Communications about jobs and travels that we both experienced strengthened our bonds with one another. So too we spoke about our parents' passing as recognition that time waits for no one. The passage of time, like the waves crashing to shore, may appear to be far too trite to give credence to life's perpetual motion. Indeed, life is not trite; nor is the love that I have shared over the years with that former black-clad lad from the Bluegrass State.

Cheers to number 33!

Voices of the Past

Some Gruff, Some Dulcet, Some Outspoken, Some Affirming, Some Intimidating, Some Welcoming, and All of Them Memorable

In a career spanning over three decades and at a school that eventually I loved to call home, one cannot help but be reminded of characters whose voices still resonate to this day. This chapter is but a mere snapshot of the many people whose footprints are indelibly etched upon both my psyche and my soul. Although the names of these individuals intentionally are omitted, their voices unmistakably could never betray their personae.

From a foreign language instructor: Upon my arrival at Culver in August 1982, orientation for the faculty to commence a new school year included (for the males) meeting with CMA counselors to provide instructions for supervision of the barracks, known as BI (barracks inspector). I was assigned to one of the units in the battery, and the counselor, an imposing, retired US Army major, spewed out one military acronym after another. Since I had no armed services background, I became more and more uneasy with each unfamiliar term. Finally, I turned to a foreign language instructor sitting next to me and confessed that I was beyond bewildered and worried I could not be an effective BI. He responded, which actually quieted my nerves and made me feel more at home with this new responsibility, "Hey, man, don't sweat it. You're gonna hate all this anyhow." I thought about some of my former public-school colleagues in Michigan who would appreciate this candor. It made sense that these words were uttered from a "foreign language" man. This same foreign language instructor's voice could be heard at a faculty meeting when he brought to the administration's attention that it was fitting to have a Culver ring bestowed to those who served for twenty-five years. However, he unabashedly pronounced, "It would be a nice touch if a diamond could be placed in that sucker (ring) for those who served forty years." No one would ever mistake this fellow for his timidity. I chuckled on more than one occasion listening to his glib retorts.

From a science instructor: Sitting in the dining hall under the mezzanine for lunch with several colleagues from across the campus, a conversation arose describing a rather large number of personnel who were new to Culver. Some of my colleagues were attempting to decipher to which department some of these new folks belonged. Some even suggested that by mere appearance, they could hazard a guess where these new people fit into Culver. A few colleagues actually knew some by name and could recite professional backgrounds of the new hires. Finally, this science instructor, after puffing on his cigarette (yes, smoking for adults was allowed at this time on campus, and even more surprising to me, it occurred in the dining hall), abruptly stated, "I never bother to learn any names until they have been here for at least ten years." Initially, I thought that this was a bit callous, but I came to realize that in many cases, people came in and out of Culver like a revolving door to a store's entrance. Later when I became a department chair, and after exerting countless hours and days to help a new instructor become acclimated to Culver, only to learn that he or she would be leaving after one year's service, I came to appreciate that science instructor's audacious remark. I continuously reminisce about a classic reference from a favorite movie of mine, *Stand by Me*. Friends come in and out of our lives quite frequently. Somehow, thinking about people as friends, tempered the callousness.

From the athletic office: Following one of those erratic and somewhat disorganized basketball practices, a fellow assistant coach and I did a double take and shrugged our shoulders as if we had heard the most unimaginable. A few dedicated players lingered for prolonged free throw shooting, and amid the quieting din of the gymnasium, one of the coaches alerted the rest of the staff that he was leaving town to finish some errands. He inquired if any of us needed anything from Plymouth, where he was headed. Without a moment's hesitation, one of the coaches replied, "Yes, could you pick me up a pair of brown slacks?" Then just as hurriedly, he left the gymnasium, and the rest of the coaches stared at one another, wondering if he was really serious. Although this coach marched to his own drumbeat, he clearly could not be serious about one of us being his own personal haberdasher. Could he? The next day at practice, the coach asked if the brown slacks had been purchased. Yes, he indeed was serious. This year of basketball was no season on the brink, no season for the ages, and no season for any particular reason; this was a season that confirmed that strange and unusual voices were the norm.

From a science instructor: Early on during my Culver tenure, I noticed a bizarre occurrence when I walked the cracked and uneven pathways on campus. Many of these strolls to and from the academic quadrangle found students hustling and bustling toward their classes. Sometimes I found myself dodging the onslaught of cadets and coeds interrupting my own steady pace. It was a numbers game in more ways than not. Yes, numbers and numbers of students peppered the landscape, but voiced numerals could be heard, coupled with appropriate salutations. My ears digested such quips as "Good morning, 17. Have a nice day, 26. You scored poorly on your quiz, 64." The recipients of these greetings were chemistry students in this bow-tie appareled instructor's classes. I thought it unusual, if not a bit off-putting, until one day I queried the instructor as to why he referenced his students as numbers. I thought it must be related to the periodic table of elements (which still brought to mind nightmares of my own high school chemistry class). I could not have been more mistaken. This science instructor suggested that his approach to communicating in this manner was his way of showing the unique nature and rapport that he shared with his proteges. No one else on campus could replicate this numbers game, initiated by an instructor, devoted to his students. I wondered if the instructor also retained a number for himself. Perhaps 007?

From the athletic office: Some coaches notoriously possess rather crude language when dealing with their athletes. In fact, I have heard it said that coaches may have saltier tongues than naval midshipmen. That said, one of my coaching colleagues joined me and a group of my Russian history students on a spring break excursion to the former Soviet Union in 1990. As it so happened, this was one year prior to the fall of the USSR. This also was the first time that this colleague had traveled overseas. I must confess that this two-week adventure proved most illuminating for my students and me for a multitude of reasons, not the least of which was listening to "astonishing remarks" from this colleague.

For purposes of literary decency, I take artistic liberties with my descriptions of such commentary. Upon arrival at Moscow, a chartered bus drove us from the airport to our hotel, located in the heart of the city, not far from Red Square. The March weather was dank, and snow mixed with sleet, cold temps, and gray everywhere we looked; the gray hue described not only the weather, but the landscape and brick and mortar buildings as well. Several large, broken-down trucks appeared to be left on the side of the highway with no drivers in sight. While on the bus ride, my colleague abruptly proclaimed, "I think I just woke up from a 1940s black-and-white movie." I knew we were headed in an alternate universe when that voice sent embarrassing shivers down my spine.

Later during that trip, all of us flew on Aeroflot Airlines from Moscow to Pyatigorsk, in southern Russia. Since there was open seating on the plane, all of us were scattered throughout the aircraft. Upon takeoff, I detected that same obtrusive voice bellowing, "Horvath, I am going to kick your behind!" When I peered toward the rear of the main cabin, I noticed my colleague sitting between two rather rotund babushkas. Both of these gals were smoking and infringing mightily upon the seat space afforded to my colleague. I recall chuckling to myself and thinking this was one heck of a way to initiate a neophyte to international travel.

Countless other examples of colorful language punctuated this trip, but one final excursion might sum up well this memorable spring break.

After leaving Pyatigorsk, Russia, we embarked upon a stay in Tbilisi, Georgia. Georgia, as is well-known, was the birthplace of Joseph Stalin, the ruthless Soviet dictator who followed Lenin in power in Russian/ Soviet history. We arrived, again by Aeroflot flight, and I learned from one of our guides that a large crowd had amassed, threatening to tear down the statue of Lenin in the city center of Tbilisi. Our hotel was situated about ten blocks from this statue. Once all of the students were safely in their rooms, I encouraged my colleague to join me in viewing this historical event in real time. I had a video camera a parent had loaned me, and for whatever reason, I fashioned myself a photojournalist. Not speaking a word of Georgian, I tried to extricate myself from a police officer who held a gun to my back. My Russian fluency was getting me nowhere fast since the Georgians were not too fond of the Russian/Soviet rule. My colleague's voice, now filled with trepidation, uttered, "My God, we are both going to be killed before we can get home."

A peaceful resolution to this episode occurred when several Culver students, defying my instructions to remain in their hotel rooms, followed us to the city center. Amid the massive, angry crowd, I was able to convince the Georgian police that we were American tourists with the help of three Culver cadets, dressed in typical American blue jeans. The night came to an "intoxicating" conclusion with all of us sampling Georgian wine from the back seat of a police vehicle.

Upon our return to Culver, a brazen voice proclaimed, "Let's plan another rollicking trip for next year." I shall provide you with one guess as to whose voice that was.

From a foreign language instructor: During my first year at Culver, I found myself still attempting to acclimate myself to boarding school life. Frequently, the campus scenery beckoned me to stroll leisurely on the walkways outlining the northern shores of Lake Max. Tranquil waters quelled my anxieties as I had grown accustomed to lake life from my native Michigan youthful days. Unquestionably, apprehension accompanied many days of that first year. On one such day, I crossed paths with a veteran foreign language instructor who must have sensed my uneasiness with boarding school life. In the most unassuming yet reassuring manner, this fellow advised, "Young man, I have some valuable guidance that I would like to provide you. Whenever you walk on campus, make certain that you always carry an open book with you. You will appear scholarly, and people will leave you alone." For months following this discourse, I carried an open book when walking on campus. I don't think anyone mistook me for being intellectual, but I did find that people took notice of my fascination with reading. I ceased this exercise except for those awkward occurrences when I wanted to avoid a protracted dialogue with someone. At a moment's notice, I could extract a newspaper, biography, or student essay from under my arm. To this day, when I see anyone gazing at an open book while walking, I think about that foreign language instructor and his penchant for avoiding people in conversation. I speculate that people glued to their iPhones are now more in vogue than being transfixed by a work of nonfiction.

From an English instructor: One automatically assumes that an English instructor would be the logical person to speak and write grammatically correctly. Indeed, this fellow possessed all the requisite attributes of one who proudly adopted formal English language. Additionally, his sartorial attire splendidly revealed that he shopped at Brooks Brothers rather than JCPenney. Students and faculty alike, from across the campus, knew this man of impeccable taste and refinement. His distinct heavily throated, deep voice earmarked him as scholarly yet sympathetic. Due to his own hearing difficulties, he tended to speak more boisterously than the normal pitch of his colleagues and students. On more than a few occasions, I could detect both frustration and kindness when he said, "My God, Joe, these students can't read. They can't write. How were they admitted to Culver?" In the next refrain, he would utter, "He has no concept of the English language, but he certainly has a good heart. How could I possibly flunk him?" Therein lay the disposition of an instructor who encouraged rigorous efforts from his students, yet he unconditionally loved them. Was he wildly popular during his tenure at Culver? Absolutely, without question! His life tragically ended in a manner replicating a character from a William Faulkner (his favorite author) novel. Before his premature death, he left an enormous imprint upon the English Department and throughout the campus. That raspy, guttural voice most likely is still remembered fondly by the many alums who once sat in his classroom.

From twin Chinese students: In the academic year 2000–01, two of the most remarkable students (and people) enrolled in my advanced placement government and politics classes. The year prior, these boys, at the age of fourteen, entered Culver as high school second-classmen (high school juniors). Their facility with the English language was marginal during their first year. However, by the time that I became acquainted with them, they attained the ripe old age of fifteen during their senior class year, and their competency of the English language was remarkable. I recall one of their peers in the AP government/politics course commented, "We are never going to beat these people, are we?" She was referencing the fact that no matter how diligent the American students were preparing for the demands of the class, they simply could not measure up to these Chinese lads. She could not have been more prophetically accurate in this particular case.

Early in the semester, these cadets approached me in my office, wanting to inquire about an unrelated course issue. One of the fellows usually spoke on behalf of both. He said, "Mr. Horvath, my brother and I are perplexed as to the nature of Culver students forming relationships that are more familial rather than collegial." Utilizing terms such as *perplexed, familial,* and *collegial* convinced me that their diligence in mastering the English language had paid huge dividends. I pondered their question momentarily and then suggested that many Culver students develop family-type bonds in activities that extended outside the classroom environment. I recommended that engaging in a sport, a club, a play, or a group might be worth consideration to gain greater insight into the familial nature of boarding school life.

The year progressed with outstanding achievements and performances in the classroom by both of my Chinese proteges. They even hosted a mock 2000 presidential debate for the entire student body in Eppley Auditorium. Both of them participated in numerous activities to include track and field and the chess club among others.

During the final week of the school year, they asked if they could visit my home because they wanted to gift me with a Chinese wall hanging representing warmth and hospitality. They also brought one of the musical compact discs that I had given them and asked if I could play one of the tracks on the CD while they visited. I obliged. The track that they selected was "Time to Say Goodbye" by Sarah Brightman and Andrea Bocelli. All three of us listened to that selection together, and then we paused the music. These soon-to-be graduates inquired if I recalled their question about familial relationships at Culver at the beginning of September. Of course, I did remember. They said in unison, "Mr. Horvath, we now understand more about familial ties because it is very difficult to say goodbye to you." Those words and those voices penetrated me as much as the Brightman/Bocelli rendition of the song itself. The marshmallow within me once again revealed itself: eyes watering and heart beating a bit more quickly.

Two days later at Culver's commencement exercises for the class of 2001, I embraced both of these shining stars. This time, my eyes were not the only ones drenched with teardrops; the waterworks dripping from their own eyes answered that sought-after response to their question. Family!

From a preacher to a teacher: Graduation weekends at Culver, replete with pomp and circumstance, are occasions needing to be lived to gain an appreciation for tradition, for appreciation, for recognition, and for sheer emotion. Having lived thirty-four of these weekends, I can attest that Culver does itself proud in pulling out all the steps for such pageantry. Beyond all of the outward displays of careful orchestration of events, however, are meaningful exchanges between faculty/staff and graduating seniors.

One such exchange developed at the Sunday morning outdoor commencement exercise for the class of 1990. As many faculty members often embrace their students to demonstrate appreciation and affection, I followed suit with seniors I had taught that year. In particular, I heartily hugged a young man whom I came to know and appreciate for his own spiritual awareness and its embodiment toward others. I whispered in his ear, "Comrade, make certain that you have a good life." He grabbed me even more tightly and retorted, "Mr. Horvath, you've got it all wrong. It's not 'have' a good life. Rather, it's 'live' a good life." The student far excelled his instructor in wisdom and in deed.

Fifteen years later in Scotland, I met this young man again. He was now an ordained minister for the Church of Scotland. Together with his wife and four small children, we celebrated his birthday and his continued wise counsel of others. As I bid him adieu and walked away, the colleague who had been traveling with me to Scotland suggested that I turn around and glance at this preacher. There he stood, as if in formation, with a respectful salute reminiscent of his final days at Culver.

From an assistant naval counselor in Upper Camps, summer school: I had the pleasure of working with the summer school program for four summers during the 1980s. Teaching tennis on the sunbaked tennis courts for one summer was enough for one who possessed a strong distaste for heat and humidity. One summer as the transportation officer in charge of ensuring that hundreds of students arrived and departed from Chicago's O'Hare Airport was maddening. Countless evenings I sat on my living room floor, attempting to match together siblings and cousins with a scattering of passports and tickets (before the age of modern technology that might have facilitated this process more expeditiously).

The first two working Culver summers found me as the counselor for Naval Two Company. I never could have fathomed what I was about to experience. I rarely thought of myself as an extremely competitive fellow, but vying for excellence in naval, athletic, and military contests became justification for many counselors and assistant counselors to claim "superiority" for the six-week summer session. Many hired staff for summer displayed a fervent love for Culver, and they looked forward to their six-week hiatus with wild anticipation. I even recalled hearing some personnel refer to the winter school at Culver as merely a perennial interruption between summers. Some of the staff could lay claim to having served Culver for more than four or five decades.

This was not the claim of my assistant counselor in the summer of 1984. He was entering his senior year of college, and he had "gone through the ropes" the previously summer with another head counselor. The two of them apparently had the same zeal toward winning because I sauntered into my role with many watchful eyes wondering if I possessed what it took to extend the excellence of "Super Two" Company. My assistant informed me that he could handle all the military components of room inspections and drills and marching. That suited me perfectly well since I had no aptitude for such components of the Culver Summer School Upper Camp. One early morning when the assistant was forming up the midshipmen for ranks to make their way to breakfast, I returned a salute from several saluting midshipmen. My assistant quietly confided to me, "Joe, we are not searching for long, lost sheep." I countered with something about the rising sun obstructing my view, so I was shielding my eyes. I don't think anyone in the vicinity bought my explanation. It may very well have been the last time I saluted anyone during summer school.

Русский язык

(Russian Language)

Attending high school in Michigan during the Cold War era of the 1960s, I vaguely recollect a statistic that appeared eye-popping to most of us. Some researcher suggested that the Soviet Union possessed more teachers of English than the United States counted students of Russian. I do not know if that served as the impetus for high schools throughout the country to begin instruction of Russian, but I was fortunate enough to attend such a school. Everything about that Cold War era reflected competitions between the USSR and the USA, from military hardware to the race for space, the Olympic games, technologic breakthroughs, and every aspect of society conceivable to the two adversaries. Can any of us, who lived through this time period, forget that Cheshire cat grin of Nikita Khrushchev proclaiming that he would "bury us"?

It was within this backdrop of history that I entered high school in 1964 and selected Russian as my choice of language study. Actually, I enrolled in both German and Russian for my freshman and sophomore years but continued my studies of the Slavic-tongued language for all four years in high school.

Initially, the thought of mastering that imposing-looking alphabet alarmed me. The teacher during my freshman year reassured the class that once the alphabet was mastered, the rest of the language would flow as smoothly as the Don (a river in the Soviet Union). He was paraphrasing the novel *And Quiet Flows the Don* by Mikhail Sholokhov. He bolstered our confidence by suggesting that the alphabet could be mastered in about a week, and quite honestly, if I recall correctly, he was fairly accurate in that estimation. Both of my high school Russian language teachers provided stimulating yet challenging lessons that inspired me to continue the study of Russian in college, both undergraduate and graduate schools.

As mentioned earlier during my initial Culver interview with Dean Alexander Nagy in 1982, I believed that he took vigilant notice of my background in Russian language and saw a future opportunity for me to become a part of both the History Department and Foreign Language Department. In the late 1980s, indeed this came to fruition, and I would characterize this time period at Culver as one of my most professionally and personally satisfying. I reveled in straddling one foot in the House of Clio and the other plunging into the world of foreign tongues. The variety of teaching in two distinct but tangentially related humanities disciplines, as well as encountering colorful colleagues in both history and foreign language along the way, doubly enriched my Culver experience.

Much like my freshman year of high school, I found myself endeavoring to allay the fears of students who grappled with the Cyrillic alphabet. I too projected that within a week, most of the alphabet would be mastered and students would "coast," not necessarily flow, like the Don. Perhaps with the passage of several decades, and this time not necessarily being inspired by such a dynamic instructor, let's just say that many students needed more than one week of study for mastery. Nevertheless, I enjoyed witnessing the broad smiles of students when they experienced success with both the alphabet and basic communication phrases. Much as all of my Russian teachers and professors had done, I too allowed students to select a Russian name by which to identify. From Boris to Natasha (no, not of the cartoon *Bullwinkle* fame), this simple exercise introduced the class to a Russian identity. The students jested with one another about their newly acquired forenames, but they also took pride in them, at least within the Russian classroom setting.

Initial lessons for beginning students included basic introductions; simple questions that answered who, what, when, where, and how; familial relationships; and geographic literacy. More advanced lessons in subsequent years would eventually lead to an investigation and study of Russian history, literature, and culture. Quite honestly, the higher the level of Russian instruction, the more intensive the lessons became. I suspect that this was a truism for learning most foreign languages. At some point in time, greater emphasis was placed upon skills that allowed students to communicate in pragmatic situations. For instance, being able to travel independently by train or airline schedule, registering at a hotel, or ordering meals in a restaurant would be useful for any speaker in a foreign country. A unique but effective lesson included students selecting a city or region and then inviting them to serve as a tour guide for that location. Effective presentations demanded research of local attractions, visual aids to complement the project, and of course, utilization of the requisite vocabulary and phrases that enticed visitors to vacation or consider a business trip to these spots. Moscow, Leningrad (later returning to the former St. Petersburg), Vladivostok, the Crimea, Siberia, and the Urals were popular choices for the advanced students.

One of the circumstances heightening my pride occurred as Culver students pursued further Russian language, history, and culture studies in college. In some cases, a few studied, traveled, and worked in Russia (the USSR ceased to exist in 1991), thereby intensifying their competency in the language. Undoubtedly, many of them have surpassed their Culver Russian language instructor in fluency. When the student excels the instructor, then the lessons were well worth the rigorous efforts!

At this juncture, I would like to acknowledge a few Culver loyalists to the cause of Russian language study. Can you believe that a few stalwarts worked with me all four years of their Culver experience? Heather Wilson, Ryan Mayfield, and Scott Johnson, all Culver graduates from the class of 1994, survived and thrived the torturous demands from Comrade Horvath. In all seriousness, the four of us bonded in times of struggle and times of frivolity. Although I do not possess all the historical academic records of Russian language students at Culver, I would offer this conjecture that these three were the only students to complete four years of study in Russian. The one exception to this would be Travis Kososki, a 2002 CMA graduate from Kazakhstan, who worked with me independently in Russian for four years.

A more humorous level of Russian study developed in the early 1990s when a significant number of faculty and staff inquired about learning Russian. Such was the narrative when twenty faculty and staff, across the campus, signed on to early morning Russian language study. At 7:00 a.m., three days a week, before the class day would commence, these eager students, with fresh cups of coffee in hand, delved into the world of all things Russian. At 7:00 a.m. in Indiana Septembers, the sun has already revealed itself, and bodies are in motion. But 7:00 a.m. in Indiana Decembers are a tad different, with no visibility of sun and bodies still attempting to remove themselves from their cozy beds. In all actuality, the intent to learn was genuine (although one instructor dropped the course after the first lesson, for which I never allowed him to forget his inauspicious early disengagement). Culver began to enroll a few students from Russia in both the winter and summer schools, and this, in part, motivated some of the adults on campus to pursue the study of beginning Russian. I applauded the desire, if not the final result of adult Russian study. To my chagrin, the course only lasted one semester as one by one, the faculty and staff followed suit of that fellow who dropped the course after one lesson. It couldn't have been the fault of the instructor, could it? More than likely, it may have been. The truism that languages are best learned when younger is probably verifiable. Perhaps I needed younger faculty and staff!

When all was said and done, I enjoyed that semester of adult Russian study even if my comrades did not. Humor, camaraderie, and exposure to the "Russian bear" all contributed to the amusement of the times before the cock crowed.

Although the class of United States history for the nonnative speaker was not included within the Foreign Language Department, one episode in this course did correspond to a bit of Russian levity. I opened this course by reminding students, whose homes punctuated nearly all parts of the globe, that we would conduct the lessons in English. Part and parcel of the course expectations was to help students enhance their English skills through a study of United States history. Since I spoke neither Spanish nor Korean, the two languages that were most prominent among these students, the steadfast rule was "English only." As it so happened, one of Culver's first Russian students was a young lady from Moscow whose English facility was meager at best. Early in the semester, she politely raised her hand and while speaking in Russian inquired about terminology unfamiliar to her. To expedite the lesson, I answered her in Russian. Latin American and Korean students took exception to my assistance to this young lady. They exclaimed, "Mr. Horvath, you emphasized only English would be accepted in this course!" In jest, I acknowledged their objection by revising the policy to one in which only English and Russian would be allowed to be spoken. I don't think these students accepted my humor, but that one lone Russian coed seemed to appreciate my concession.

One of my great laments during my Culver tenure was witnessing the elimination of the Russian language course offerings. Fewer and fewer students enrolled in Russian, and in fact, fewer enrolled in a number of foreign languages. This brought to mind that we in the United States approach foreign language study far too belatedly. I would encourage schools throughout the country to initiate language pursuit in the lowest of elementary grades. Unquestionably, I would be partial to Russian, but whatever the foreign language that a school district selects, it seems logical to continue with that language throughout all twelve years of school. Chinese, Arabic, Spanish, and Russian are vitally important in today's globally connected world. However, I continuously advised all of my students in government, history, and Russian that they should include a foreign language in their college course curriculum. Sometimes, selecting a foreign language not particularly well-known, such as Serbo-Croatian or Uzbek, might prove useful in locating a position after college. Bilingual or trilingual global citizens will find that they have the world at their fingertips. For a few years at Culver, I took delight that my Russian students held a world of possibilities within the grasp of their own fingers. I closed this storied chapter of my life with a fond remembrance of all those people who inspired me and hopefully whom I inspired to study Russian.

A Priest in the Making

Oh Danny boy, the pipes, the pipes are calling
From glen to glen, and down the mountain side
The summer's gone, and all the leaves are falling
T'is you, T'is you must go and I must bide.
But come ye back when summer's in the meadow
Or when the valley's hushed and white with snow
T'is I'll be there in sunshine or in shadow
Oh Danny boy, oh Danny boy, I love you
so. (Lyrics to "Oh Danny Boy")

The above Irish (although composed by an Englishman, Frederic Weatherly) classic references a parent bidding adieu to the son going off to war. It has long been a favorite of mine because the lyrics authenticate the cycle of life. People perpetually enter and exit our lives. Some quickly pass as when day turns to night. Such was the case with Daniel Patrick Ketter, better known to his family and friends as Dan, and more affectionately referred to by me as "Danny."

Three Shots of Vodka and Eight of Water

Have you ever met someone who, simply by knowing him or her, made you a far better person that you ever thought imaginable? I met just such a fellow in August 1992. The faculty intern program at Culver, now into year number nine, brought us eleven eager faces. The dean of the Academies hosted all of these gentlemen at the local pizzeria to launch the new school year. "Deano," an institution of and by himself and a Mr. Chips clone, devoted tireless energies into molding the faculty intern program into the enormous success that it became and remains so to this day. On this particular August evening, I found my way to the local pizza parlor, having recently returned from a trip to Florida for my niece's wedding. I intruded on the dean's soiree by offering an introduction and a welcome shot to Culver. My intentions were generous if not my pocketbook. I discovered that I had enough cash for only three shots of vodka (in keeping with my Russian mantra). Hence, the order to the bartender was to pour three shots of vodka and eight of water. The predictable reactions of our eleven recipients revealed who gulped the Stoly and who settled for the aqua. I apologized to the eight and of course to the dean for my intrusion. I think that I even promised to buy a shot for the eight before the year concluded.

Such were the circumstances that allowed me to come face-to-face with Danny. Initially, all eleven of the group appeared as if they belonged to the same college fraternity—frat boys, if you will—and were neatly groomed, prep attired, and athletically inclined. Danny distinguished himself as particularly outgoing. His welcoming handshake, broad smile, and wry wit appeared to draw others in the group to him. However, something inexplicable separated him from his peers. I discovered in the coming months what that something was.

Dean, Where Are the Roman Catholics?

In the history of Culver's faculty intern program, I have been blessed to have worked with many talented and dedicated recent college graduates who wanted to learn more about teaching. Unquestionably, I could write a book about these teaching neophytes and the service for several decades that they have provided our school. From 1989 to 1992, the good dean assigned three superlative young men to work with me in the History Department. I learned considerably more from these fellows than they ever did from me, which explains, in part, why I have been so fond of this program from its inception. I became better at my craft when working with people who brought enthusiasm and insight from their college campuses. The uniquely common thread of "my" interns from the previous three years? Jewish, one and all! I jested with the dean and inquired, "Where are the Roman Catholics?"

In 1992, he obliged me; well, he almost did. John McCann, an Irish Catholic fellow from the East Coast, and I connected as a team in the classroom and as friends outside the academic setting. In fact, we remain in contact today, usually via Christmas cards. However, he would sheepishly classify himself as a "fallen away" Roman Catholic. St. Mary's of the Lake, in the town of Culver, was the residence of our local pastor. This priest, an intriguing man, and the most secular priest whom I have ever encountered, reputedly laid claim to fame for his sermons. Perhaps I should say the brevity of his sermons. The students at the Academies referred to attendance as "MacMass," parroting the Sunday exercise as fast-food service. If his sermon would ever exceed ninety seconds, one began to gaze at his watch in disbelief. To our clergyman's credit, his messages from the pulpit were unmistakably clear, pertinent, and poignant.

At a particular September Sunday Mass, I exited St. Mary's with one of the English Department interns. Danny, the outgoing intern at the pizza parlor, and I joined one another for breakfast at one of the local cafes following our "Mac Mass." We chatted extensively about our own Roman Catholic upbringings and even a bit about the role of the church in the world today. I intuitively sensed how vitally important his faith was to him and came away from that conversation uplifted and encouraged. I felt uplifted because he heightened my own spirituality and encouraged because he offered hope for the younger generation to appreciate the relevance of organized religion. I had often been criticized for allowing the temporal world to dominate my spiritual one. Since I engaged frequently in political discussions, these assertions could be justified. Nonetheless, my genuine interest in and passion for Roman Catholicism would be cultivated more deeply by and through contact with Danny. For the remainder of the school year, we often attended Sunday Mass together and actually started several weekdays by going to Mass since our teaching schedules allowed us to do so. After all, if one thought that Sunday "Mac Masses" were fleeting, one can only imagine the length of a weekday Mass!

Bam-Bam, a Birthday, and Pebbles

When I was forty-two, my first malady of any kind hit me like a rock. A kidney stone attack left me as physically vulnerable as I have ever been. While in the hospital, a nurse informed me, "Mr. Horvath, I have experienced both childbirth and kidney stones, and the pain of childbirth is not nearly as severe." I imagined, "How comforting!" After six weeks of doctors' visits and tortuous pain, I too gave birth to a sharp-edged, definitely not so precious stone. My colleagues in the History Department had proclaimed on the chalkboard in the office, "Joe is proud to welcome Bam-Bam to this world!" Danny served me as both personal servant and spiritual advisor throughout the ordeal. From raking leaves and retrieving groceries to offering prayers for recovery, I came to rely upon his kind benevolence.

When the raking ceased and snowflakes began to descend upon us, the time to celebrate two birthdays in one arrived. John, my own History Department intern, and Danny shared the same birthday of December 4. Danny's colorful and dynamic English Department mentor and I planned a dinner celebration at the Tippecanoe Restaurant, and former home to the Studebaker family, in South Bend, Indiana, befitting both guys. It may have been the spinach salad, the filet mignon, Philadelphia cheesecake, Long Island iced tea, beer chaser, or a combination of all of them, but the birth of my second kidney stone, Pebbles, occurred later that evening. The two interns thought that I was celebrating their birthdays, but in reality, I simply rejoiced in being kidney stone free. Free at last. Little did I comprehend then that I would do battle with stones countless times over in the years ahead.

Demon Deacons versus Spartans

Danny, a graduate of Wake Forest University in Winston-Salem, North Carolina, was a native of Atlanta, Georgia. He spoke with no southern accent, was not a fan of NASCAR or redneck humor, and boasted never about Confederate supremacy. Truth be told, he possessed strong Midwest stock. Born in Seattle, Washington, his family's roots germinated in Minnesota and South Dakota. I mention this merely as evidence that Danny could well have originated from any section of the country or the world for that matter. His gentle and warm disposition transcended region and geography. One would be hard-pressed to detect any sort of excessive pride with this most humble soul, unless the subject of college athletics arose. Make no mistake. My Roman Catholic buddy matriculated to the land of demons—Deacons, that is. It seemed anomalous that he enrolled at a school that traced its lineage to the Baptists in 1834. On second thought, perhaps becoming a Deacon was nothing more than a pit stop on his life's journey.

Wake Forest would never be mistaken for an NCAA football powerhouse. It was no USC, Alabama, or Notre Dame on the gridiron. However, Danny's competitive juices burst onto the scene when basketball season arrived. We entertained many a debate about the prowess of his Demon Deacons and my Michigan State Spartans, his ACC (Atlantic Coast Conference) and my Big Ten Conference. Surprisingly, our two schools never competed against one another in basketball, but it mattered not since we were ready to challenge one another about the supremacy of the boys from Winston-Salem and those from East Lansing. For many years (and I secretly still do today), we kept score of which conference performed better during the NCAA version of March Madness. More recently, the ACC-Big Ten challenge provided face-to-face, heated battles, and I have been left with more egg on my face than he has on his. Nonetheless, if one of our teams or conferences excelled, religion seemingly entered the fray with crusade-like chants of "God wills it!" The signal was becoming more and more unambiguous to me: Danny's days as a "Deacon" were numbered.

From Telluride to London

Travel is inherently every Hungarian gypsy's delight! During Culver's February winter break, Danny, Jeff Kurtzman (another intern), and I flew to Rocky Mountain high country in Colorado for a ski weekend. Some dear friends and some of my favorite Culver parents, Tom (CMA '60) and Val Mortell (I taught their two sons, Tom Jr., CMA '86, and Jake, CMA '90), invited us to the quaint Victorian ski resort of Telluride. Home to the famous film festival in early September, Telluride captured every skier's fancy with powdery snow, rugged peaks and moguls, chairlifts at nearly every descent, and a hot tub awaiting aching muscles after a day on the slopes. Aside from Jeff's air sickness on the flight from Denver to Telluride, and coping with heavier breathing at the higher altitudes, the three of us enjoyed the respite away from the academic routine of a Culver winter. Danny, the most expert skier among us, reveled in the challenges of soaring down the mountain from heights only angels seemingly could ascend. Jeff, the novice, took to cross-country skiing, and to the best of my knowledge, he has continued his interest in this sport to this day. As for me, this was the last time that I ever set foot on a snow-capped mountain, and I have no particular valid reason why this was so.

On the return flight to Indiana, we openly and excitedly spoke of another travel adventure. Rome and the Vatican captured our imagination. Would a more apropos trip exist for two "roamin' Catholics?" Even Jeff, who is Jewish, appeared intrigued by such an expedition.

Following spring break, Danny and I did think about a European adventure, but Rome and the Vatican took a backseat to what we envisioned as a fitting conclusion to Danny's Culver career. For the life of me, I simply cannot remember why we dispensed with Rome as a travel destination. Instead, we focused upon the British Isles, and more specifically England and Ireland. I spearheaded the itinerary for England, and Danny penned the same for Ireland.

During the summer of 1993, the two of us flew from Atlanta, following a colleague's wedding in nearby Athens, Georgia, to London. London is by far the most cosmopolitan city I had encountered. I loved this metropolis, have returned several times, and the city on the Thames remained high on my list of favorite spots in the world. The Theatre District, sprawling gardens, royal palaces, pub crawls, black taxis, and tube connections only added to the ambiance and excitement one experiences when visiting.

Traveling by train to Canterbury, Cambridge, Stratford-upon-Avon, and Oxford punctuated our English journey. Danny, not surprisingly, focused our Irish mission upon cathedrals, monasteries, shrines, and oh yes, a few pubs. After all, Danny surmised, "Roman Catholics dabble in more than sacramental wine." The Ring of Kerry and the Rock of Cashel highlighted our trek through the Emerald Isle. We promised each other that our next trip together would be Rome and the Vatican. (As a postscript, Danny has made several trips to the Eternal City, all without me. I finally visited in the summer of 2019 with none other than a Mormon. Go figure.)

I returned to Culver, a bit saddened, knowing that Danny would no longer be joining me for Sunday Mass, an NCAA basketball game, eating a meal together, or watching *Thirtysomething* (a dramatic, four-year television program) episodes on television. Danny was searching for new occupational challenges in entrepreneurial business. I indicated that I would support him in whatever decision he made regarding his

Danny and I, Sunday mass companions

future, but a viscerally strong reaction told me that he probably would continue to search for future endeavors. Somehow, I could not envision him in the world of business. John D. Rockefeller, Andrew Carnegie, Bill Gates, Warren Buffet, and Danny Ketter seemed ill-fitting.

Discernment

Contemplative, deliberate, and careful would be apt descriptions of Danny. I never witnessed him acting or behaving impulsively, and as such, whenever we scanned a restaurant's menu, shopped for a pair of shoes, or planned an excursion, I could rely upon two or three or even four revisions as not being extraordinary. Sometimes I would chuckle to myself; sometimes I became impatient or even agitated; sometimes I would vacillate between the two. Eventually, I came to accept that Danny's decision-making processes required time, tolerance, and reflection.

Danny carried this innate quality into his teaching at Culver. His mentor instructor, a master in the classroom and wildly popular with his students, agonized for Danny whenever lessons needed preparation. The two could not have been a study in greater contrasts, yet they held each other in high regard. Danny's innocence and dedication would evoke nothing but esteem from others. I recall on one occasion when Danny asked me why he rarely saw me preparing lessons for my history classes. He caught me off guard with that inquiry and caused me to ponder why I treated the preparation of lessons so cavalierly. Perhaps I had become stale with my own teaching. Perhaps I needed to reexamine why I initially had become a teacher. Perhaps I needed to follow Danny's example and plunge myself into my work. Good teachers inspire their students to ask, "Why?" Danny inspired me to ask myself, "Why?" If Jesus was the ultimate teacher, Danny certainly was His disciple, deliberately following in His footsteps.

On many other occasions, I recollect asking Danny if he ever considered life as a cleric. He attended one of the premier Catholic high schools in the country at Atlanta Marist, and he remained especially close to several of the priests at his alma mater. It seemed logical and appropriate that he would follow in many of their footsteps. With contemplative, deliberate thought, Danny did enroll at Mount St. Mary's Seminary in Emmitsburg, Maryland, many years after leaving Culver. We sporadically did communicate with one another over the years, and as one can imagine, he wrestled with his decision to first become a seminarian and eventually a priest. Only he can understand and fully appreciate his own discernment. I was so honored to be invited to his ordination on May 31, 2008. Seven other seminarians in the Diocese of Atlanta were also being ordained that weekend, but naturally my eyes and attention were focused upon the fellow who entered my life in 1992. I observed him as one with the same engaging disposition and warm smile that punctuated his countenance while at Culver, with one notable distinction. Danny had heard the pipes calling him, and he answered that call at long last.

I continue nightly to pray for Danny in his role as a parish priest and recognize that his presence in my life, albeit far too brief, was a gift from God. I asked Danny, when the time arose, if he would consider celebrating my own funeral Mass. He willingly obliged and informed me that he could have a lot of "fun" with his eulogy for me. In the event that he would neglect to mention it, please, let the record show that he made me a better person—far better—than I could have ever imagined.

A King and a Queen

King, Eleanor, and I at Culver's Christmas Dinner Dance

We pride ourselves in this country of a society without royalty and espouse a de jure egalitarian nation. Thoughts of an esteemed nobility, majestic coronations, and visions of Camelot exist merely within our wildest and most fanciful imaginations. Yet upon my entrance to Culver in August 1982, I came face-to-face with a "regal" couple who, for all intents and purposes, became my mentors, my adopted parents, and my king and queen.

After a stint in the US Navy as a mine sweeper in the Pacific during World War II, and subsequently completing his degree in history at

Tufts University, Lewis Kingsley ("King") Moore signed on to teach at Culver in the fall of 1952. Disdaining following in his father's footsteps in the world of business, he sought a career of inquiry, research, and scholarship. The lure of New England was not enough to prevent him from planting his educational seeds in the rich soils of north central Indiana. A bachelor upon his arrival in 1952, this gentleman whetted his appetite in boarding school life and lapped up every morsel of nourishment that Culver had to offer. For four years he lived the life of a history instructor, guiding Culver's cadets through Western civilization. Diligently preparing rigorous lessons, with occasional interruptions of watering hole visits with his fellow bachelor comrades, would be a routine that altered considerably when he returned to Culver in the summer of 1956 with his bride, Eleanor.

I only know of the legendary stories from the early years of this pair because they shared them with me during the time that I came to know them. Suffice it to say, the two were different from one another in a multitude of ways. One was supremely knowledgeable about the historical world; the other was completely informed about the latest gossip in town. One whose travels led to museums and cathedrals, while the other's destinations included bargain basement stores and a farmers' market. One became intoxicated by novels of antiquity, and the other was engrossed with jigsaw puzzles. Living together in a world of contrasts, however, did not diminish the love that these two had for one another. King and Eleanor raised two charming daughters, each grown and away from home by the time my life intersected with theirs.

King hired me to teach in the History Department at Culver in 1982, and my ten years of teaching in Michigan's public schools could not have prepared me for what I was about to experience. Opening orientation meetings overwhelmed me, in large part, because Culver utilized a language all its own. In particular, acronyms and terms used for and by the military personnel confounded me. BI, CCQ, OCQ, and Tattoo were the proverbial Greek to me. I became more and more uneasy as the meetings progressed and contemplated more than once why I left my native Michigan. Optimistically, I thought someone finally would break away from all the formality of these opening sessions and the welcome door to Culver would open for me, if only but a crack. I stepped through the threshold and would keep my eyes and ears open for anyone who might offer guidance to help me survive year one. It should come as no surprise that King would be the one providing me assistance, wise counsel, and friendship, all prerequisites for success in a new job. I was grateful for that opened door that King held for me. I learned also that an opened door required me to walk through it. I did so with a degree of trepidation and a flicker of hope.

As previously mentioned, King's East Coast origins (both Long Island and Boston) served as quite a contrast to Culver's rural "corn silk curtain." He brought with him an unquenchable thirst for scholarship. If ever I met anyone who loved history more than he, I would be hard pressed to ascertain who that someone would be. In fact, many of my colleagues within the History Department surreptitiously coveted the scholarly crown that King modestly wore. Most, however, were unwilling to exert the laborious efforts of study that King envisaged as necessary for success in and out of the classroom. One can only imagine the unsuspecting student who did not acquire the "armor" requisite for historical battles in King's classes. Those who did became all the more enlightened for the intensity and passion that they developed as a result of sitting front and center in King's seminars.

Inexplicably, King and I were drawn to one another at first glance. He interviewed me during the lazy, crazy days of the summer of 1982, and we found a mutual interest for Russian history. At the time of that interview, I was fascinated with a high school that appeared more akin to a small, liberal arts college campus. Seventeen hundred acres on the northern shores of Lake Maxinkuckee, a campus that housed imposing structures with gargoyles adorning the classical architecture of its academic buildings, and including its own golf course, airport, and horse stables with hippodrome, ice-skating rink, and chapel with heaven-reaching steeple, all overwhelmed me. Where was I? I thought I must be dreaming. The sailboats that glittered the lake, the small aircraft that exited the runways, the horses that galloped the vacant grassy fields, and so much more seemingly caught my fancy more than conversations I engaged during my interview. This was akin to no high school I had ever witnessed.

King took time to interview me between the summer school tennis lessons that he was teaching during Culver's summer school program (a six-week venture into the world of adventure and exploration for students from ages nine through eighteen). It is often referred to as a camp, but rest assured, the roughly 1,400 "campers" who matriculated to the summer program returned home with proficiency in horseback riding and jumping, sailing, aviation, and countless other sporting and leisure activities. King sat with me under a welcomed, shady, old oak tree as he perspired from the previous tennis lesson on the sunbaked tennis courts. I remember thinking how unconventional this interview appeared. However, the informality and ease with which King and I conversed immediately allayed some of the angst that I was feeling on the drive from Michigan to Culver. I liked King immediately, and I think that the feeling was mutual; at least, I hoped that was the case. It was a sharp contrast to my meeting with the dean of the Academies, Alexander Nagy. I recognized that the surname Nagy was Hungarian, just as mine was, so I thought that we would share one thing in common. Upon reflection, I think that was the only thing we did share. He was formal and imposing, yet he commanded a great deal of admiration from most on campus I was later to learn. What is surprising about this initial interview is that although the vacant position was in the History Department, there was an added attraction: my Russian language background. The former Russian instructor had become blind and left Culver years earlier, and I think Dean Nagy saw me as a possible replacement down the road within the Foreign Language Department. Following interviews with both King and Al Nagy, an invitation to become part of the Culver Academies faculty came almost immediately—the next day in fact. I applied for a position in the spring of 1982, in large part to start a new life. For reasons, unmentioned here and now, I wanted to leave Michigan, and Culver extended me the opportunity to start anew. I leaped at the chance.

First years of any new profession are replete with unexpected challenges. My initial year at Culver fit the norm. I arrived with ten years of teaching experience in Michigan public schools, yet most of the faculty I met that beginning year had multiple years, if not decades, under their belts at Culver or were neophytes just out of college. The footprints that I would follow seemed to be in neither category.

Early in the fall semester, King and his wife, Eleanor, hosted an evening cocktail party for many of their friends in their third-floor apartment (a six-apartment building reserved for the most influential and veteran instructors on campus). I knew King, of course, and a few others, but this provided me with my first encounter with Eleanor, who was the "queen of campus information" because she made it her business to be informed of happenings surrounding the school and town. If that is a polite way of suggesting that Eleanor knew and sometimes spread the latest gossip, I suspect that it may be fairly accurate. Eleanor held several secretarial positions on campus, and that New England accent, complete with an omission of *r*'s in every word spoken, would never camouflage her Bostonian roots. If I liked King immediately, I was intrigued by Eleanor at first glance. She glided throughout the apartment at that first soiree as if she commanded most, if not all, the attention. King, on the other hand, appeared perfectly content to allow his wife to occupy center stage.

This would be the first of countless dinner parties hosted by King and Eleanor that I attended. The requisite blueprint for each social gathering included a cocktail hour (or two) followed by a meal fit for kings and queens. Eleanor, in spite of her disdain for cooking, was indeed an excellent cook and chef. Maybe it had something to do with the fact that guests imbibed in at least three or four alcoholic beverages before sampling her carefully chosen and prepared dinners. I recall one such evening when one of my colleagues, fairly new to Culver, leaned over to ask me when food was going to be served because he was becoming slightly inebriated within the two hours allotted for cocktails. I chuckled and told him to add more ice to his vodka tonics.

As the many years progressed, King and Eleanor invited just me for dinner, and yes, of course, a few cocktails, on more than a hundred occasions. (I am certain that I do not exaggerate by that number.) In short, we became more than colleagues and friends; we became family. I knew that I was being treated as a "favorite son" within the History Department, and I honestly reveled in it. Fellow members of the House of Clio even remarked that they felt as if they held secondary status to me. King, as chair of the department, had taken me under his wing, tutored me in the rigorous demands of the discipline, and envisaged that I would follow in his footsteps as gentleman scholar. I sharply recall in one of his evaluations of me that he saw great potential as someone who demanded diligence on the part of his students that would help them stretch their own academic muscles. At the time of reading such an evaluation, I was proud and humbled to receive such an accolade from the person I most respected in and out of the world of academia. Years later, I recognized that I could not hold a candle to the gentleman scholar King embodied. I may be utterly biased, but I suspect Culver has never employed a greater giant in his respected discipline than Lewis Kingsley Moore. His name aptly describes the man: King.

In her own way, Eleanor also treated me as an "adopted son." She showered me with thoughtful gifts at Christmastime and birthdays. One summer school colleague suggested that in his afterlife, he wanted to return as a son or grandson of Eleanor because of her generous gift-giving. No one was a greater shopper than Eleanor. She could sniff out a sale from miles away. Toto (a nearby town with discounted items, the likes of which would make Sam Walton of Wal-Mart fame sit up and take notice) became a frequent haunt of Eleanor's. If King could spend his perfect day while reading Plato's *Republic* and listening to Tchaikovsky's *1812 Overture,* then Eleanor's perfect complement would be to search for the sales of a lifetime at Filene's Department Store in Boston or the drastically reduced bargains from neighboring Toto. Unmistakably, these two were quite a pair, and I came to love each of them for their own unique attributes.

Certain events in our lives earmark milestones that serve within the lifelong recesses of our minds. For many of us at Culver such an event was the shocking passing of our dean of the Academies, Alexander Nagy, in October 1994. Dean Nagy, in addition to serving in a major leadership role, taught one section of advanced placement United States history. All administrators at Culver taught at least one academic course to keep them front and center within the curriculum of this college-preparatory school. Dean Nagy taught this same course for decades prior to my arrival, and he and I shared the same basement classroom within the confines of the Memorial Legion Building. The Roman catacomb-like appearance of the basement replicated the annals of history and served as an ideal environment to discuss events from the rise of the Renaissance to the Louisiana Purchase. Upon learning of Dean Nagy's death, the campus absorbed a pall-like atmosphere, and from which many years afterward, the school still bereaved one of its giants.

Nagy arrived in 1956, and his devotion to Culver and lifelong bachelor status is likened to Mr. Chips, from boarding school fame. In particular, I was affected directly by this tragic event: I assumed the role of taking over Dean Nagy's AP US history course. This extra course, in addition to my own teaching assignments, provided more challenges than I was able to meet satisfactorily. How could I possibly replace this pantheon's imprint that the legendary Alexander Nagy carved during his tenure? I could never fill his shoes, and that would be a painfully difficult lesson I learned the hard way. I mention this monumental event in Culver history because of the dark cloud lingering for many months and years afterward.

That said, however, there was another event that had an even more profound impact upon me, and it occurred two years earlier in 1992. The closing of that school year marked the retirement of both King and Eleanor Moore from Academy service. The History Department hosted a grand party celebration for both King and Eleanor, and the commendations for both came from far and wide across campus as well as from former colleagues of theirs, most of whom I had never met. Once again, I stood in awe of this "King and Queen" as so many wished to extend their gratitude for these East Coast transplants. This time, the pall created by their vacuumed absence from campus life left me adrift. My mentor was no longer sharing the House of Clio with me. His wife was no longer the communicator of information, keeping me updated on campus life. My world had changed, and how was I going to navigate these new trepidatious waters? My frequent dinner visits with these "adoptive parents" continued, but I now found us engaging in different conversations. To be sure, we appropriately consumed both history and wine with each meal. However, I assumed the roles that King and Eleanor had played: resident historian who was wrestling with curricular changes within the department and provider of campus small talk. The latter proved particularly daunting for me. Eleanor surely was disappointed in my lack of understanding the importance of the latest faculty news. Upon close reflection, I did not execute either role very well. How could I? After all, I was following in the footsteps of a "king and a queen"!

International travel served as connective tissue for King and me. WWII in the Pacific might very well have been the beginning of exploration for King, but European ventures dominated most of our conversations. Our shared interests from ancient Greece and Rome to the feudal systems of medieval Europe, the rise of nationalism and totalitarianism in nineteenth- and twentieth-century Germany, and Russia whetted our appetites to experience history through travel. Although King and I never traveled together as companions, our conversations about museums, cathedrals, battle sites, landscapes and seascapes, and pubs and restaurants revealed such narrative similarities that one would have assumed we were travel mates. Many of these conversations ensued well into the wee hours of night or early morning, some even with a few cocktails to enliven those discussions. Eleanor usually called it an evening once talk turned away from shopping. In hindsight, I think I was not as considerate of her as I should have been. I regret that. Nevertheless, some of the best times of my life were spent engaging my mentor about travel, history and culture, languages and peoples, and aspirations for future globetrotting endeavors. To this day, whenever I am traveling in Europe, I cannot help but think about King and wish that I could share those experiences with him.

In 2003 my own mother would turn ninety years of age. With my siblings' assistance, I planned an elaborate surprise birthday party for Mom with relatives and friends, with over 150 attending. The planning and preparation for this festive occasion were months in the making. Eleanor, always at the ready for the grandest of parties, gave me some ideas that would delight my mother. Eleanor and King had met my mother on a couple of occasions, and although Mom was just a few years older than they were, all three seemed to become fast friends. I like to think that it had something to do with me. I suspect it rather had more to do with the life experiences that they shared.

It always seemed to me as if the Great Depression of the 1930s shaped mindsets and perhaps even lifestyles for those who lived through this era. Perhaps I am oversimplifying this notion, but Mom liked the Moores, and they liked her. It was for this reason that I wanted my dearest friends and "adoptive parents" to be with me at my dinner table for Mom's ninetieth. It was not to be.

June 21, 2003, and one simple telephone call to Michigan considerably altered life for so many. King called to tell me that Eleanor had passed away. My heart broke for him, for Barb and Bonnie (their daughters) and their families, and for me. As it so happened, Eleanor was buried on King's seventy-ninth birthday and two days before her own eighty-fourth birthday. I still can close my eyes today and reimagine King struggling so bravely, almost heroically, to eulogize his partner in life at the quietude of the Culver Cemetery gravesite. The tears that welled up in his eyes were replicated one by one by the rest of us mourners. God bless you, Eleanor. If there is a shopping sale in the afterlife, I know to whom to turn to discover its location.

The weeks, months, and years following Eleanor's passing indeed were fraught with emptiness. King and I still met for drinks and dinners, not quite so often as before. Somehow that empty chair in the dining room on Liberty Street, with its memories so vibrant, so chilling, and so full of love, became a poignant reminder of an absent queen. One important dinner with King did occur in the autumn of 2003: my mother's surprise ninetieth birthday extravaganza. I did not have any expectations that King would attend solo, now that Eleanor was gone. He did arrive, however, and he seated himself next to his "adopted son." Most assuredly Eleanor smiled upon both of us that evening.

There did come a time when I am not altogether certain that Eleanor smiled so benevolently upon her mate. Several years after Eleanor's passing, on a brisk autumn day, I found myself exiting the Academies' post office and running head-on with King. He wanted to show me something, so I waited for him to collect his own mail.

Sheepishly, he pulled out a photo of someone I did not recognize. I peered at the picture and asked if I was supposed to know this lady. He coyly smiled and related that her name was Frances, someone with whom he had become acquainted on the European cruise he recently undertook. Still a bit perplexed, I must have appeared utterly naïve to King. Frances, an English literature aficionado, another world traveler, and a Texas-bred gal quite unlike Eleanor's New England lineage, first became King's lady friend and subsequently his second wife. I came to realize, largely based upon the insights of one of my female humanities colleagues, that it was not that unusual for an aged widower to assume a second marriage. She suggested to me that women, by in large, are stronger emotionally than their male counterparts. Men who lose their female partners are more apt to seek someone to fill the lost emotional attachment they no longer possessed. I thought about my colleague's assertion, and although I am not confident that this paradigm is entirely accurate, it might indeed have some validity. Well, it certainly seemed to in King's case. What I remember most about this newly discovered scenario is that Barb and Bonnie, King's daughters, related to me that King would have "hell to pay" when he left this earth and met once again with their mother. I chuckled when I first heard this. I think they were correct.

On July 30, 2011, King did indeed pass from this earth. He had no longer been living in Culver, having moved to Frances's native Texas and then Arkansas. My interactions (and many others at Culver as well) with King diminished the last few years of his life. I am hopeful that he spent many happy days away from his legion of Culver faithful. A memorial service for King in October 2011 at the Culver Memorial Chapel allowed those of us left behind to pay their respects and share their adoration for Lewis Kingsley Moore IV, a Culver man and a Culver legend. I was honored to speak at this memorial service by providing King's eulogy. Most assuredly, any words that I spoke would pale in comparison to the greatness that King exemplified throughout his storied life. The lyrics of "Ye Men of Culver" during this service never carried with it more significance. King was the epitome of a Culver man.

Much like a chessboard now absent its king and queen, my initial thoughts reflected game over. Years later, and with appreciable objectivity and clarity, I realized that the game of life is never over. The king and queen live on in Culver lore, in family hearts, and in me.

Al, We Hardly Knew Ye

We all have come to know people who perplex us. They may camouflage their inner selves, are inherently introverted or extroverted, or have an inexplicable manner, among the many other reasons. One of Culver's giants, Alexander Nagy, confounded me more often than not. Allow me to set the record straight. I am not suggesting that all Culver constituents did not know Dean Nagy. What I offer, however, is that few, if any, knew the man well. He provided mere glimpses of who he was and what he represented. A cloak and dagger investigator might find him to be a challenge of a lifetime. Certain factual evidence is difficult to refute. Dean Nagy arrived in Culver in 1956, served as a unit counselor, history instructor, and dean and principal of the Academies, among many unofficial capacities. His untimely death in 1994 brought his Culver career to its unseasonable conclusion. Between the years of 1956 and 1994, Dean Alexander D. Nagy's mark upon Culver history was unmistakably etched for thousands of patrons to memorialize. Just precisely what that mark reflects was contingent upon each patron's perspective. The following is merely one such perspective.

I met Dean Nagy in late June 1982 when I arrived for the on-campus interview for an instructor's position within the History Department.

His matter-of-fact demeanor initially appeared a bit off-putting. Clearly, he was all business, and my attempts to infuse our conversation with some basic Hungarian phrases *(Nagy* and *Horvath* are both Magyar derivations) flew out the window. I spoke laconically as the good dean capsulized the history and nature of the school. The entire interview could not have lasted an hour, and I found it challenging to get a read on this fellow who inquired little of my background. The most memorable comment from this meeting was when Dean Nagy excused himself to use the restroom by stating, "I need to powder my nose," before introducing me to the department chair, L. K. Moore. I thought it odd that a man would use this expression, but I mentally filed it away as boarding school jargon of which I was unaccustomed. I do recollect that Dean Nagy hurriedly concluded our interview.

I would learn much later that he was impatiently anxious to embark upon his summer interlude to "the Farm" at Stanford. He usually spent the entire month of July in California, escaping the "down-home Midwest charm of Indiana." Perhaps this was the primary reason that I was offered a position at Culver within twenty-four hours of my departure and return to Michigan. It could not possibly have been that I impressed anyone by my initial contact. Years later, Dean Nagy confessed that he was intrigued by my background in and facility with the Russian language. At any rate, I was offered and eventually accepted the position within the History Department, which was the most prudent professional decision of my career. In my mind, Dean Nagy would remain a mysterious fellow for the next twelve years.

Most of what I learned about Dean Nagy stemmed from sharing a classroom in the bowels of the Memorial Legion Building, where the History Department was situated. Not surprisingly, we in the House of Clio referred to these digs as the Roman catacombs, especially when the spring rains arrived and the corridors and classroom floors were submerged with the flooding waters.

Observing the good dean in the early morning hours of each classroom day afforded me some opportunity to witness his work ethic. I reminded myself on more than one occasion that Dean Nagy had been teaching one section of advanced placement United States history for decades. His yellowed notes indicated as much. Dean Nagy's commanding stature in front of the classroom and his anecdotal lecture references earmarked him as popular with many of the most academically gifted students. When I began teaching the same advanced placement course, I discovered that many of my students were disappointed that they were assigned to my section. Some of these students were Culver legacies whose fathers, older brothers, or uncles had been taught by the legendary Nagy. How could I compete with such a renowned figure? Why would I even attempt to do so?

Never more did this visceral reaction become apparent than when I assumed Dean Nagy's section of history upon his sudden death in October 1994. The entire campus was in a state of mourning, and his own AP students bore this grief as profoundly as any of us. Dean Nagy's administrative responsibilities obviously took precedence during his professional life. As a result, and I mean no disrespect when I share this, I never considered him a scholar of history, as I would come to view several other of my colleagues in the History Department. I cannot recall a single conversation when Dean Nagy and I spoke about a historical novel, political perspectives of past or current historians, or research that revealed different or revised views of America's past. Coincidentally, although I could speculate about his own political leanings, we never once engaged in any historical and governmental discussions of merit. His close to the vest political orientation transcended to many facets of his life. It seemed as if he wished to represent "everyman," the stock character in fiction. This protagonist's benign conduct would allow the readers to identify with, and consequently accept, him. Quite honestly, this is how I deemed Dean Nagy wanted Culver constituents to perceive him.

Kentucky Derby Day was the one day that Al Nagy would select as his own birthday. This became emblematic of his own cryptic nature. He adamantly referenced that his birthday fluctuated between any dates in early May whenever Churchill Downs dominated the headlines. It became only evidentiary when his own obituary revealed that May 2,

1933, was the date on his birth certificate. Certainly, many of us know people in our lives who wish to camouflage the actual dates of their births. That is of no great surprise or shame. However, Dean Nagy guardedly protected his own identity. One could theorize the many possibilities for such an approach to covert existence. I would be one of the last to hypothesize or provide accurate rationale for Dean Nagy's reticence to share more of himself. I recollect Dean Nagy meeting members of my own family at a Sunday parade, and my father thought that since Nagy was of Hungarian descent, he might greet him with a simple "Hogy van?" ("How are you?") In the brief exchange that was conducted in English, my family and I learned that Nagy traced his origins to upstate New York. In fact, he was raised in the same small town where my sister-in-law was born. When I queried him about growing up in the northern stretches of the Empire State, his taciturn response indicated definitively that it was time to change the subject. Rebuffed, my initial reaction to what seemed an innocent inquiry solidified my view of Dean Nagy as puzzling. Over time, I accepted that our conversations would not extend beyond the superficial. Additionally, he referred to me less as "Comrade Joe" and more as "Uncle Joe."

Nicknames can be adopted as replacements for unwelcomed monikers bestowed upon us at birth. I had no nickname until I arrived at Culver. Somehow, students attached "Smokin'" or "Comrade" to my first name, Joe, to humor themselves more than me. I graciously acknowledged and indulged their levity. Dean Nagy must have overheard "Comrade Joe" on occasion because he did reference me as simply "Comrade" in my early years at Culver. At some point in time, he began calling me "Uncle Joe." Initially, I thought that we Hungarian descendants were stretching our familial bonds. Gradually, I came to appreciate his reference as affirmation that I was no longer this wandering gypsy from the Great Lake State. At one History Department "cookie night"—a monthly evening gathering that included socializing with conversation about a historical topic or book or an invitation to a guest speaker that served as professional development in the truest sense of the concept—I referred to Al Nagy and others who taught only one class in the department as "interlopers." I thought I caught his wry smile aimed toward my direction; rather, he was revealing his disgruntlement of my description of "part-time" members within the House of Clio. Somehow "Uncle Joe" no longer seemed so familial.

The references to uncle did continue, but usually they were followed by inquiries of my venturing to South Bend on the way to Michigan. I could deposit Dean Nagy at the South Bend Airport to catch a bus to Chicago for a weekend leave. On several occasions, I drove him to Chicago to trade life inside small-town America for the Windy City. One would think that two hours in a car would elicit meaningful or memorable conversations between us. I honestly cannot recollect a single one of those talks. I would add that Dean Nagy, not possessing a vehicle or holding a valid driver's license, seemed peculiar to me. Hearing rumors (none of which were confirmed) about him being involved in a sports car fatality only exacerbated the intrigue surrounding this "interloper." Hence, his reliance upon walking underscored that a headmaster's path in boarding school life can be restricted in multiple ways.

Dean Nagy's vibrancy was most discernible within two components of his responsibilities. The first was with alumni during the annual May alumni weekend. The second was the faculty intern initiative that he and Dean Ralph Manuel launched. I actually witnessed a lilt in his step just prior to the third weekend in May as many of his former charges (and many who were not) would acknowledge their gratitude for his guidance during their high school years. He was masterful in recalling minutiae about these folks, so much so that he could recall what row and seat they occupied in his classroom. Further evidence of his attention to detail would be his ability to recite their hometowns, their family members, their extracurricular activities, their college alma maters, their spouses and children, and their occupations. I stood in awe of his uncanny capacity for recollection. Perhaps even more consequential was that he warmly welcomed each of these alums back to the "home" that shaped their youths and their futures. Yes, Dean Alexander Nagy was indeed a Mr. Chips of his time.

The second facet of his life that brought him great joy was in helping to promote and celebrate the faculty interns. His vision for expanding such an enterprise cannot be marginalized as today, Culver still can proudly boast about helping young college graduates inaugurate their professional careers. His frequent attendance at the local pizzeria (Papa's) would find him entertaining these interns with stories of bygone days, sports trivia, or upcoming Culver events. I once suggested that he had invested stock in Papa's Restaurant because of his persistent patronage. Following his death, the owners of the restaurant hung a plaque to honor and memorialize their good friend and customer. I took comfort in knowing that with alumni and interns, Dean Nagy experienced many happy times. I wondered if other aspects of his life and job allowed him such joy.

I am not certain that Dean Nagy was a packrat, but following his death, and with the considerable help of several Culver constituents, his artifacts were collected, inventoried, and subsequently distributed to many of us. I personally received the Christmas cards and letters that I had penned for him during our twelve-year association. I learned that thousands of blue book essays written by countless numbers of students were retained, perhaps for posterity. Maybe, just maybe, it was the historian in his soul that he could not depart with what would become a part of his history, the legacy of a counselor, History Department instructor, administrative dean, and Culver man. Denison, Northwestern, and Stanford played integral roles in Dean Nagy's life, but none of those prestigious universities could rival Culver in magnitude and commitment. No history of the Academies could ever be written without the inclusion of Alexander Nagy's varied contributions.

I do not wish to appear so audacious that I boldly pronounce for all at Culver that they too hardly knew the man whose left arm resembled a Napoleonic posture. Apparently, Dean Nagy crushed his elbow from a tumble while rushing to an appointment along the notoriously steep sidewalks in the Nob Hill section of San Francisco in the 1970s. One colleague informed me that his arm was nothing more than a "coat hanger" from that point forward. The perpetual image of him holding on to his coat jacket is one that is embedded within my memories of him.

Perhaps this depiction holds similar recollections for others. I suspect that some affiliated with Culver, particularly those who knew him for decades, may have known and understood this celebrated figure more than I did. However, I do believe that most of us might reiterate, "Al, we hardly knew ye."

Fun and Games
Gone Awry

Practical jokes have intrigued me for most of my life. Usually, I found myself on the butt end of those jokes, and as long as they were delivered in a good natured manner, I took them in stride. Occasionally, the jesting could be hurtful or mean-spirited, in which case I endeavored to veer from such bantering or activity. An enterprising cadet in one of my classes was notorious for his pranks. I always found them innocent enough, but I did caution him that one day someone on the receiving end of his well-intentioned humor might take exception. He listened to my cautionary advice, but I am not certain that the words fully resonated with him.

As it so happened, in the spring of this cadet's first class (senior) year, I learned of a major infraction that involved him. This type of error in judgment could well have resulted in possible dismissal from school. I liked this young man a great deal, but I decided that perhaps the shoe should fall on the other foot, so to speak. My intention was to put the fear of God in him just long enough for him to recognize that he might be living a little close to the edge of skirting Culver rules and regulations. I crafted a hurriedly typed note that requested this cadet visit the commandant's office to discuss the possible infraction and had it delivered to his mailbox through the Academy postal workers. I shared this covert operation with his roommate, who thought it would serve my intended purpose of shaking up the fellow. Both young men were in one of my afternoon classes, and I instructed the roommate to bring his pal to the classroom after the academic day rather than having him proceed to visit the commandant.

When both cadets attended class, I could not help but notice that one of them appeared as white as a ghost. He was nonparticipatory, and his countenance suggested that something was amiss. As class concluded, I winked at the roommate to solidify our rendezvous in a few hours when all the classes had concluded for the day. That said time arrived, but no cadets materialized. I wondered what had happened to alter the colluding scheme between the roommate and me. Fifteen minutes elapsed, and the roommate, utterly out of breath, came rushing to my classroom. He gulped his words as if he were swallowing his last meal. Initially, I had difficulty understanding what he was attempting to say. When he calmed down for a few minutes, he informed me that he could not persuade his pal to come to see me. He insisted that the young man was going to throw himself on his sword and confess his rule violation to the commandant.

I felt a rush of adrenaline and dashed across campus as quickly as my leather penny loafers would propel me. In hindsight, I think I slipped once or twice on the heavily cracked sidewalk along the way. As I approached the commandant's office, I observed a young man seated outside the office, with his head bowed in hands. I leaned in next to him and suggested that we needed to converse with one another back in my classroom. Initially, he resisted, but I was able to convince him that what I had to communicate was vitally important. When we returned to my "home turf," he placed his head down on a student's desk, without even a glance my direction. Soberly, I confessed to him of my prank and asked for his forgiveness because I never intended to cause him such additional stress that he apparently was experiencing.

The words "I'm sorry" barely exited my lips when he lifted his head and pointed his index finger in gun-like fashion while proclaiming, "Gotcha, Mr. Horvath!"

Bewildered, I retorted, "What do you mean?"

He replied, "My roommate told me of your devious plan. You should have understood that the blood is thicker between roommates than it is between instructor and student."

I had been ambushed, played, double-crossed, snared, and whatever else one might reference for such a sneak attack. What a prank! I yielded to these conniving cadets because they played the game better than I had.

I uttered, "Touché! Please don't forget that I know something that the commandant does not yet know." With that simple retort, I wiped the smirk from the face of the cadet seated in front of me.

Over the next couple of months until graduation weekend, my car was washed impeccably several times. Additionally, my apartment appeared cleaner than any cadet's spit-shined shoes. It was amazing how compliant this cadet became when I requested a few service projects.

He unabashedly grumbled, "This is blackmail!"

I acknowledged his assertion by suggesting, "I know it is, but let's not call it that."

Graduation weekend arrived, and when it came time for faculty and staff to congratulate the seniors and first classmen, I embraced the culpable cadet and whispered in his ear, "Pranks can take many twists and turns. Thanks for reminding me that he who laughs last laughs best."

His reply eerily sent a shiver down my spine. "Mr. Horvath, I have now graduated. Keep your eyes open at all times."

We parted ways, broadly smiling at one another. They were the smiles of fun and games gone awry.

Letting Go and Holding On

First Day of Class—August 2009

In a state of flux, I began my twenty-eighth year at this illustrious institution along the placid shores of Lake Max. The tumult of the previous school year had taken its toll. My ninety-five-year-old mother had died in April, and it was apparent to all those who knew me that I was struggling with the grieving process. A priest friend of mine had told me that it would be some time before I would be able to go forward without thoughts of loss dominating my everyday activities. A colleague had suggested that I needed to "reinvent" myself. Each of my siblings attempted to deal with the loss of our mother in his or her own quiet way. All I could comprehend is that I was lost and alone. As with so many of us who have experienced the death of the final parent, I came to think of myself as an orphan. I knew that I was not ready to begin a new school year with the enthusiasm and excitement that an instructor should bring to the classroom. Coupled with the fact that the Humanities Department (the History and English departments) had merged to become one, members looked to me for guidance and support as their department chair. I was certain that I could counsel and advise no one (student or teacher) with much success.

My advanced placement government and politics class commenced with two engaging young men occupying the front table of seats. Nothing particularly distinguished them from the other sixteen students, except that both fellows shook my hand when the class concluded. I remember thinking that this was a nice gesture and perhaps reassured myself that maybe I could still find some passion in teaching eager and respectful students.

Day two of class arrived, and these same two students replicated what they did on the first day. Their eyes, wide-open to new vistas, and wry smiles suggested that they enjoyed their experiences at Culver and life itself. Since both cadets ranked at the top of the leadership chain, their active engagement with one another underscored their trust and friendship with each other.

The subsequent days and initial weeks progressed in routine fashion: smiles and laughter throughout each class, followed by a firm handshake to bid adieu.

My normal approach to breaking the ice with any new group (especially students) was to invoke humor. I recognized fully that my sense of humor bordered on the cynical, but for the most part, it helped me overcome a natural tendency to be reticent with the unknown. I also knew that being able to recall every student's birthday was another mechanism that I could employ to bridge the gap of unfamiliarity. Most of the students did not quite know what to make of such an accumulation of trivia. Actually, one of my colleagues, Andy Strati, suggested that this is all that I did know. He was much closer to the truth than I wished him to be. I learned this game of birthday recall from my mother, who remembered to her dying day all significant dates of births, weddings, and deaths of those close to her. She once related to me that remembering people's birthdays was akin to showing them how much they meant to you, how important in life they were. She displayed grace and generosity in doing so, and I could only pray that someday I might emulate her thoughtfulness of others.

Monday Nights at the Huff

One of my duty assignments was to serve as library proctor every Monday evening in the Huffington Library. Ostensibly, all a proctor must do was to help maintain good study conditions for the students. As I had come to appreciate, however, this duty had the transparent advantage of being able to work with students in an individual academic environment. Of all my duties at Culver, library proctor remained my favorite because of this distinct privilege; I could help students who wanted or required it.

Cadets Canacci and Hunnewell learned that their teacher, Mr. Horvath, would be willing to work with them early on in the school year. Every Monday night the three of us labored together about the nature of federalism or structure of the White House office or the complexities establishing health care reform. During the second semester when the course turned from United States government to comparative government, the issues became far more cosmopolitan as we debated the merits of parliamentary versus presidential forms of government or neocorporatism dominating a state's ability to govern independently.

Occasionally (perhaps more often than not), our attention was diverted to other issues of the day: namely, leadership at Culver, athletic practices and competitions, girlfriends, selection of colleges, religion and morality, and the aspirations of eighteen-year-olds. Although one cadet was more gifted academically and the other was more inclined athletically, they connected on the same level in almost any facet of life. Through these Monday evening rendezvous, I knew that a special bond existed between the two. The fact that I began to share some of this bond caused me to reflect upon my own experiences as a high school senior. (I had been an introverted and unworldly teen, naïve about most of his surroundings.) We developed a level of confidence with one another and knew that our words, perhaps our emotions, would be safeguarded much as within a priest's confessional.

At one of these Monday night study sessions, these two leaders of CMA began to talk about a European excursion after their Culver graduation and prior to matriculation to West Point. The more that they spoke of such an excursion, the more intrigued I became about their plans. I suggested that they needed a chaperone and perhaps I could accompany them. Surprisingly, both of them seemed eager to have me "intrude" upon their "brotherhood" exploits. The two musketeers would become three. Athos, Porthus, and Aramis would be resurrected!

Alas, the European grand adventure would not occur due to their reporting for summer duty at the United States Military Academy, but the very thought of planning and preparing such an undertaking excited all three of us and cemented the bonds of a trio alliance.

Early Morning BRC and Weekly Lunch Dates

Eating with the regimental staff on a regular basis served as another unifying venue. Part of my dietary restrictions involved eating more oatmeal and drinking more orange juice, and since I rose early each morning, sometimes in the middle of the night, it became more than happenstance that I would eat with Cadets Canacci and Hunnewell. They consumed every breakfast food imaginable except when they were in wrestling season and attempting to cut weight. Sometimes we continued our conversations from the previous day or evening. Sometimes we explored new territory such as both of them explaining to me the significance of operations on the boys' side of the school. Here I was, a Culver veteran of nearly twenty-eight years, and I could only entertain the foggiest notion of the traditions of Culver Military Academy. I learned all that I know today about the honor council, promotions, and parades from these two cadets. They even bestowed upon me the bars of a regimental commander, which became prominently visible on my own coat. (I did receive some rather strange looks from some of the military mentors.) Clearly, I recognized why they catapulted to the front and center of their class and this school.

I had worked with many superlative cadets in the years previously spent at Culver, but the esprit de corps that the two of these gentlemen shared appeared unmatched. Sometimes one of the three of us would miss a breakfast "meeting," and somehow the rest of the day seemed incomplete, almost unacceptably so. We might even resort to commentary that would put the absent "musketeer" to shame. Nonetheless, the good-natured jabbing served as further evidence that esteem and affection punctuated this holy triumvirate.

Shot Glasses, Bagpipes, and Rugby

What an odd assortment! My undeserved reputation as a hard whiskey drinker unwittingly evoked an unexpected response from the students. Initially seeking postcards from students who vacationed to exotic and not so exotic lands during spring break, I received a bevy of shot glasses from all over the world. Cadets Canacci and Hunnewell had begun this enterprise by giving me shot glass souvenirs from New York City, purchased during a New Year's Eve celebration. This gesture repeated itself many times over following spring break as many of the other classmates followed suit. Ah, yes, our CMA leaders in action! They surely were the locomotive engine that pulled this train.

I had heard bagpipes when my colleague Andy Strati and I had visited Scotland four years earlier. The melodic, almost haunting sound caused such a stir for both of us that we perched on a park bench in Edinburgh, listening to a piper blow the Scottish Highland tunes. I knew that one of my protégés was committed to playing the bagpipe, but until I heard him play for the first time, never could I imagine that I would be so proud of knowing such a musician as he was. His talents as scholar, leader, and athlete were now supplemented by his pipe artistry. During alumni weekend, when I saw him lead the corps of cadets on to the parade field as regimental commander and then seamlessly switch gears as a pipe soloist, I understood well that his talents were limitless.

Equally talented, but on a different playing field, my other protégé excelled as a star rugby player. His kicking ability distinguished him from his teammates, but more important, his passion for the sport infected and inspired vast numbers of Culver boys to play a game that should be reserved for men—burly, muscle-bulging men at that. When I saw the rough and tumble nature of these competitions in all sorts of inclement weather (I confess to watching some games from inside my car), I came to appreciate the commitment and physicality that these players must possess to compete. I still had no concept what the rules entailed or how scoring occurred, but I did know that I was equally proud to witness this star in action. I suspected that many would hear of his rugby triumphs at West Point and beyond in the coming years.

Music, Music, Music

I love music! No, I mean real, meaningful music! Honestly, doesn't everyone? Music supposedly represents the universal language of all.

I have absolutely no musical talents whatsoever, but you might say that I appreciated the melody, the harmony, and the lyrics of most songs. Now, the "music" of the last several generations offered certain challenges for me. More aptly stated, I didn't quite understand how much of rap or hip-hop fell into the spectrum of music, but I suspected that the same was uttered by my parents' generation when they rolled their eyes as I listened to the Beatles. Here is where technology received high marks. I could send, via YouTube, video clips of the music and lyrics of the pop performers of the fifties and sixties. This was my generation's contribution to the fabric of American society. My heart sang with each clip that I sent to my two cohorts, and my countenance brightened when they informed me that the songs were "sick." (Sick in the good sense, an expression lost on me because I was generations removed from their dialectic lingo.) John Denver singing "Follow Me" and Bob Dylan's "These Times Are a Changin'" are timeless for any generation, and my proteges not only recognized this but affirmed their kinship with me by doing so.

February 19, 1992, and July 28, 1991

Alexander Grant Canacci was born on February 19, 1992. Blake Harrison Hunnewell was born on July 28, 1991. My mother taught me well. Birthdays of those whom we love are to be remembered. I am fairly certain that I could follow in my mother's footsteps for Alex and Blake. I convinced myself that she was grateful that these two cadets helped lessen the mourning period for her son. That priest friend of mine who randomly appeared in and out of my life reminded me once again that saying goodbye to a loved one is one of life's most difficult moments. I repeatedly confided to him that it is so difficult to let go. He coyly smiled and once again asserted, "Joe, you keep forgetting that the letting go is the easy part. It is the holding on which is so difficult." You would have thought that I would have both understood and internalized these words by now. Apparently, this was not the case; some lessons are harder to grasp than others.

Three musketeers, Alex, Blake, and I

Painting Bridges and Other Such Things

Dana's Jeep shimmied up my driveway to carry us on a secret rendezvous mission. The only instructions that I had received were to dress comfortably. Forgive me, Mother, but blue jeans were the order for the night. My mom long had hated blue jeans and thought that they were decadent, helping to foster the demise of society. Dana and I traversed the backcountry roads, making our way to Ora. How could one accurately depict this sleepy hollow, nestled in remote Starke County? Suffice it to say, Ora's one stop sign was one hardly noticeable. One might even suggest unnecessary as we did not encounter a passing vehicle along our trip down the dusty roads and paths. I must admit that it seemed out of character that we observed a palatial estate in the midst of dwellings indicating that life is a struggle for many of the inhabitants.

Dana clearly knew what the plans were. I did not. Normally, I would have been unsettled by the uncertainty of what was to transpire, but the Jeep ride conversation ameliorated my anxiety. We were looking for an abandoned railroad bridge. The instinct (my instinct) was simply to search until we found it. My colleague Dana, far more prudent than I, suggested that we stop to ask directions. My instincts were wrong. Dana's were correct. This would be only the first measure of his keen, native intelligence that surpassed mine. Dana's trusty Jeep made its way down a winding path to what most likely was a horse farm. No one appeared for several minutes, although a pack of dogs wildly barked at us intruders. Even one of the horses galloped at us when we approached the house. The property reflected a disheveled yet serene nature. After one of the dogs (we thought it might be a pit bull) danced around our Jeep, Dana suggested that the dog looked friendly enough and we should get out to rap on the door. Once again, Dana's savvy nature overshadowed my timidity.

I did finally extricate myself from the Jeep, but only after I witnessed the foreboding dog was less than intimidating and Dana was safely nearby. The owner of the property eventually exited his house, and upon first glance, appeared perplexed by these two vagabond Academy personnel. His directions to the abandoned bridge sounded a bit convoluted, but Dana nodded and assumed that I would be able to help us find our way. Instantly, I panicked, knowing full well that I only had a vague notion of what the gentleman was telling us. All of my travels throughout Europe flashed before my eyes when I usually took the wrong train at the wrong time.

Dana and I did make our way, adhering to the directional path before us. The gravel Three Mile Road was aptly named. As we neared what we thought was the river, we halted and got out of the Jeep to observe a cemetery. Only in Starke County, Indiana, would there be a cemetery in the midst of a farmer's field! The flattened and faded headstone markers gave some indication as to the protected sacredness of this piece of property. Plastic flowers adorned the markers, some of which had been unearthed and turned askew. Someone had taken the time and opportunity to show respect and love for those no longer among us. Dana and I remarked that this was a scene like neither of us had ever witnessed before. Surely, I had many visits to cemeteries, making my sporadic pilgrimages to my own parents' gravesite. However, this one was different as some rather inexplicable emotions within both of us were being awakened.

My cell phone rang and took Dana and me out of the moment,

out of the time capsule that enraptured us. My cousin Franny called to wish me a happy birthday, one week early. I appreciated her sentiments nonetheless, even more so because she was recovering from a severe stroke in an Ann Arbor, Michigan, rehabilitation center. God love her for remembering her cousin. I wanted so to speak with her at greater length, but I did not want to have this experience with Dana interrupted by an extensive telephonic conversation. Franny, one the dearest and sweetest gals to ever walk this earth, was also one of the chattiest, and I knew that the conversation could well exceed several hours. I told Franny that I would call her over the weekend, and then Dana and I proceeded to head back to the Jeep. Before doing so, however, Dana noticed a hang glider hovering in the skies to the south of us. This image, firmly etched in my mind, still seemed surreal; Dana and I gathered around a dozen broken-down headstones while gazing at the motorized glider from a distance.

The bridge could not have been more than a few hundred yards from where we had stopped at the "cemetery junction." We parked, grabbed the spray paint, and maneuvered toward the bridge. As it turned out, this involved doing some hiking up and down boulders and hills toward a new gravel path that led directly to our destination. Dana had informed me of our mission a bit earlier along the Jeep ride. We (he intended that I) would spray-paint over some graffiti that had been scrawled on the exterior of the bridge. Last summer during one of his canoe trips, he mentioned that his campers could not focus upon anything other than the obscenity clearly visible to all river travelers. Perhaps we could even leave a message of our own, symbolic of a mission accomplished.

Arriving at the destined bridge, my legs began to tremble. The slats on the bridge were weather-beaten and rotted to the core. Dana led the way, and I followed, hoping that he would not notice the fearful facial grimace with each of my leaping steps from slat to slat. I immediately observed that hanging over the iron outer edges necessitated quite a vault from the wooden slats. I know that Dana's plan called for me to press and spray the paint over the undesired obscenity. He would hold me by my ankles as I leaned over the bridge's edge. I wish that I could portray myself as brave enough to accomplish this request. Alas, I was not. Years upon years of living an ordered existence had taken its toll, and what little adventuresome spirit I ever possessed had long since dissipated. The river was not a raging one, but the flow was steady. Simply looking down the nearly twenty-five feet reminded me that I needed to look out and not down. The last roller-coaster ride of my life taught me that lesson. I wondered momentarily what was so wrong with an obscene remark on a dilapidated bridge. Perhaps I merely wanted to convince myself that the mission really did not need a successful conclusion to be considered a triumph. Maybe the mission merely entailed the recapturing of a boyhood spirit. I tried to rationalize this as a goal, but I was somewhat disheartened because disappointing Dana would be *a bridge too far to cross.*

Dana did indeed accomplish the task. All the while, I kept praying the novena to the Virgin Mary to protect him—and me. Dana asked what words should be left as our indelible message for future canoeists. I initially had told him, "Stand by me," because this evening reminded me of what it was like to be twelve again, and scenes of that 1980s film resonated throughout our Ora expedition. We decided that the peace symbol from the 1960s might be apropos and a bit easier to paint on the bridge's exterior. I took delight in knowing that when Dana did canoe the river during the summer, he may glance at that symbol of peace and reflect fondly upon our mission to paint the bridge—our mission to bond with one another. Dana tossed me the can of spray paint, and we locked arms in a spirit of brotherhood, the brotherhood that boys at age twelve come to rely upon. It underscored that twelve-year-old boys eventually become men, and the fellowship that ensues as adults strengthens that affiliation.

Scaling the peaks and valleys of the hills and back to the Jeep revealed a zip in our steps. Jumping from boulder to hill and doing so without breathing too deeply actually surprised me. The two of us could not have appeared more differently to the casual observer. Dana, recently forty-seven years of age, tanned, slender, yet muscular and eager to embrace life's next adventure contrasted sharply with a nearly sixty-year-old whose pale complexion resembled a body and soul scarred by the aging process and introspectively looking at the world around him. Yet Dana's touching and inspiring remark that he thought I was rather agile evoked a wry smile. Perhaps being "twelve" again could be recaptured, albeit momentarily.

From the Jeep, Dana called my attention to the setting sun. The skies' hues could not have been more photographic. Again, I thought, *Where is the camera?* I reminded myself and Dana that my skills as a photographer could never have done justice to what we were observing. The drive home, now completed in darkness, involved stopping for a bite to eat. I suggested that the local eateries in Culver would be closed by the time we arrived along the shores of Lake Max, so we dined at the Sportsman's Bar in Monterrey (after learning that the Corner Tavern there stopped serving food a half hour before our arrival). I should have been hungry. I was not. The night spent with my "brother" was sustenance enough. I vaguely remember that a grilled cheese and grilled chicken sandwich somehow found their way into our stomachs. Scrutinizing the pub's clientele gave Dana and me an opportunity to converse about our travels abroad. I may have uttered something akin to "Monterrey is a far cry from the streets of London."

We arrived at my house around 10:45 p.m., and I enticed Dana to come in to read something else I had been writing. I wanted his opinion. I sought his approval. Brothers do these sorts of things. Seeking approval, that is. Dana and I embraced, and his Jeep shimmied down my driveway. Hours later when my head hit the pillow, I closed my eyes and thought about the transformation that occurred in the past few hours. I thought of painting bridges and other such things. I came alive. Life once again seemed full of promise and excitement for the first time in a long while. I dreamed dreams of a twelve-year-old boy.

A Sequel

Roughly one week following this adventure, I took two of my students to the same locale that Dana had taken me. I still had that same can of black paint, and I "requested" that these guys shimmy along the edges of the bridge and spray-paint, "Stand by me, Dana." I knew that they would have a rollicking good time acting as monkeys swinging from the iron bars that traversed the dilapidated bridge. Indeed, they frolicked, and I reveled in their youthful playfulness, reminiscing of what my own youth was like long ago and far away. I had secretly hoped that when Dana took summer school campers canoeing down this river during his summer adventures with the Woodcrafters, he would gaze upon that bridge and witness firsthand that I had eventually summoned enough courage to transcribe that message of friendship to him.

When I did not hear from him over the summer, I wondered if he had not noticed that brotherly message. Upon returning on the first day of school, Dana sought me out in a crowd of instructors attending the opening meeting. He coyly smiled and quipped, "I received your message, Joe, along the front edges of the bridge, but I am perplexed as to how this was accomplished." I matter-of-factly asked why he would suggest that I could not have completed the task. He stated rather emphatically that "Dana had been misspelled as Danna." So much for me and my conniving attempts to fool him! Which one of my former students had the misfortune of not mastering spelling? To this day, I decided that I would rather not learn which of them would have never qualified for the Scripps National Spelling Bee.

Old Man, Are You Circling the Drain Yet?

In 2010 a young man sauntered into my senior American government class with an attitude that he would control the environment, academics notwithstanding. As he dominated every arena in which he entered, one could never ignore or take Austin for granted. Confident in his abilities yet undisciplined in his approach, engaging wit yet impish behavior, faking cerebral acumen yet possessing visceral reality, annoying his peers and instructors alike yet endearing himself to both of these constituencies, Austin Welch was a young man for all seasons. Early on, I was quite certain that he and I would *tangle at every angle.* Little did I know then that I would come to hold this enigmatic fellow in the highest esteem and with great affection during that year of 2010 and beyond.

Perhaps a signal that I should have capitalized upon was hearing from other instructors and staff about Austin's escapades in his first three years at Culver. From his foreign language instructors and band and orchestra instructors to his counselors came the same utterance: "Austin is a handful. His precocious inclination to skirting rules, taking short cuts, and focusing more upon mischief rather than growing from adolescence to young adulthood undermine what Culver professes within the school mission." That said, when Austin entered my classroom for the first time,

I could not help but notice his devilish smile that announced he and I would engage one another on various levels, many of which neither of us could comprehend at the time. This teacher-student relationship was ready to begin its roller-coaster ride!

Austin's utilization of iPhone technology, while discarding more traditional approaches to learning (namely, reading from the text or assigned handout readings), was merely the initial phase of our rather discordant approaches to study. I do not believe that I could count a single day of class in which Austin actually brought any study materials with him, other than his iPhone. His attention span to our classroom discussions was frequently interrupted by his incessant communication with the outside world. What confounded me most was that when I queried him about topics of the American polity, he invariably responded with answers that occasionally were both insightful and pertinent. This kid possessed enormous talent and promise, but he reveled in frivolously playing the system to succeed. Anyone who could see through many of his vapid answers knew that he exuded more hot air than substance. Yet it was most discernible to me that Austin would meet his match someday with those who would demand both detail and analysis in his academic endeavors. I regret to admit that I was not that somebody who could persuade him to intensify his efforts. Nonetheless, the two of us grudgingly yet gradually developed a mutual admiration for one another.

Meeting Austin at his level required me to resort to my own playful youth. Clearly, he was not prepared to meet me on my terrain. Austin's penchant for pranking others was not lost on me. Nevertheless, his cunning nature, seemingly an annoyance to most adults on campus, actually infected me with an attitude that this fellow needed to be taken down a peg or two. When it came to pranks, he was not playing with some amateur. I had been known as one whose own devilish nature could be just as bothersome to others as Austin's might be. Several examples illustrate the one-upmanship with which each of us countered the other.

Austin commandeered my laptop one day and sent an email to one of my classes, informing them that the class had been canceled.

To my chagrin, I could not comprehend how he managed to pull this off without my knowledge. On another occasion, during a very sultry spring day, he turned the thermostat up in my apartment to ninety degrees. Later that evening he texted me and inquired, "Comrade, are you exceedingly hot tonight? You might check the temperature on your thermostat." You might inquire as to why he even was in my duplex apartment. Austin, on many occasions, would venture to my back door, open it without knocking, and inform, "Old man, let's get something to eat. I am hungry." I understood the "old man" reference to be a sign of affection rather than one of irreverence. At least I convinced myself of this. Coming to Culver from Winnetka, Illinois, Austin and his family were not strapped financially. Somehow, however, Austin, imploring that we should go out for dinner, never seemed to have his wallet with him whenever he visited. In retrospect, I doubt that I would have ever allowed him to pay for dinners that the two of us shared. If the truth be told, I relished those opportunities to engage with him outside the classroom.

As I noted, I too could be ever the prankster. One Wednesday afternoon, during an all-school convocation, I suggested that every student and faculty and staff member bring a newspaper to the meeting. Austin, who at that time was in charge of conducting the school assemblies, was greeted with an auditorium filled with everyone holding up and reading their newspapers, rather than listening to his oratory. He knew immediately who was behind this event. Later that spring, Austin's entire wardrobe and his prized iPad came up missing from his barracks room. It wasn't too long into the afternoon when he called me and asked where his personal belongings were. He eventually received his "lost" apparel, but he learned not to "mess with the master," as I reminded him. In actuality, he was far more a master of these escapades than I was. I could not match wits with the pro that he had become in gamesmanship. Even taking his master key to campus facilities at graduation that he somehow obtained seemed anticlimactic. He played (and beat) me like a drum. Just as important, I was somewhat enamored that he did.

Less one would think that these games were predominant in the relationship that the two of us developed, I would be gravely misleading in my recounting the year that I spent with Austin. As with any relationship that grows over time, Austin and I shared personal triumphs and challenges that brought us closer to one another. He confided in me that his birth mother died tragically in an automobile accident while he was a six-month-old infant in the car. He survived, but upon learning of this event, I could not help but wonder what sort of impact this played upon his psyche as a youngster, adolescent, and for that matter, for the rest of his life. His father did remarry when Austin was a young lad, and to the best of my knowledge, Austin has come to think of his stepmother as his own mom. They have established as close a relationship as any son and mother could have. As further evidence of this bond, it is noteworthy that Austin accepts his three half-sisters as his own. There is nothing "half" in those relationships. Austin maintained and continues a deep commitment to his family to include a loyalty to all of his grandparents. His maternal grandfather died while he was a senior at Culver, and I recall our conversation with one another on the drive to take him to the airport to fly to St. Louis for the funeral. Somehow the playful Austin evaporated during our conversations that took on the reality of life and death. I felt compelled to share with Austin the circumstances of my own mother's passing, which occurred a little less than a year prior to meeting him. To this very day, Austin remembers to forward me a text that he is thinking of me on April 29, the day of my mom's death. I endeavor to do likewise on April 1, which corresponds to his birth mother's fatal automobile accident.

Remembering significant dates that serve as markers in one's life included our birthdays, holidays, graduations, and retirement. Every May 26 and September 24 (our own birthdays) highlight includes a conversation with Austin. There was one exception, however, to these occurrences. When Austin was into his second year at West Point (somehow, he "conned" his congressman into a nomination for the United States Military Academy), he neglected calling me on my birthday. I thought that our relationship may have run its course. After all, it is not that common for students to maintain a close relationship with former instructors after leaving school. Nonetheless, I did think that Austin and I had a uniquely special rapport with one another that would pass the test of time. Months after my birthday, he informed me that he was on maneuvers in Panama and was unable to telephone me. I only half believed him, but to carry forth with a bit of frivolity, I texted him a map of Panama on his birthday, insisting that I was unable to communicate directly with him. Austin later revealed that he nearly fell from his seat while in class at West Point when he received my text.

As with many students with whom I engaged throughout my tenure at Culver, Austin replicated the conservative political ideology of his own family background. Culver possesses a rich history of students matriculating to the shores of Lake Max with fathers, mothers, grandfathers, grandmothers, uncles, aunts, and cousins whose own lineage included strong business and entrepreneurial ties. Coincidentally, or perhaps not so much so, these business interests are slanted toward conservative inclinations. My personal story emanated from strong progressive values. Although as I have aged (not so gracefully, I admit), my involvement in liberal issues has moderated since those youthful days of college. Austin, like many of his fellow Culver alums, sparred with me over the role of the federal government, social policies, and economic viewpoints, among so many others. What made these highly debatable discussions unique is that Austin could match me wit for wit on topics that many other students had difficulty articulating. At the end of each discussion, we usually agreed to disagree. I think that speaks well of the respect, admiration, and esteem we maintained for each other.

Austin's academic and personal record at Culver belied what lay ahead of him at West Point. At some point (and without my personal observation), Austin matured and gained the discipline that he needed to earmark him as one of America's great young leaders. He always possessed the intellect and communication skills that distinguished him from most of his peers. West Point and those who inspired him there instilled the passion and organizational skills to garner him several awards and leadership skills that he was unable to acquire at Culver. Austin graduated from West Point as first captain of the Corps of Cadets (the highest-ranking cadets at West Point), which might have astonished many of his Culver military mentors. I would not consider myself one of those disbelieving but one who took great pride that I was privileged to have interacted with Austin while he was a Culver senior.

Austin, after four years at Culver, four years at West Point, and five years in the US Army, began working on his two-year MBA program at Stanford University. The "kid" who propelled his way to heights that perhaps even he could not have envisioned undoubtedly will serve his country and his generation for decades to come. Austin has met and conversed with political, economic, and media leaders at the highest national level since he graduated from Culver in 2010. He has spoken to civic groups, graduations, military hierarchies, and business organizations the likes of which I cannot begin to enumerate.

There have been numerous students over my forty-four-year teaching career who impressed me greatly because of their academic intellect, passion for learning, kindness, humility, and industrious work ethic. Austin was not one who neatly fit into any of these categories. For reasons that I am unable to articulate cogently, Austin is befitting of one of my most memorable students who has transformed into one of my dearest friends and proteges. As an aging retiree, I take comfort and find affectionate humor whenever Austin calls

*Congratulating Austin upon
his CMA graduation*

to inquire, "Old man, are you circling the drain yet?" One day he will call, and the lack of response from me will indeed indicate that I have "circled the drain." I think that he will have a good laugh; perhaps so shall I.

Type A, Times Two: Harry D. Frick IV and Bradford W. Trevathan

At first glance, these two colleagues and friends of mine would appear to possess little in common. One whose religion would be consumed within the basketball world of Hoosier hysteria and the other whose religion represented a conversion to Judaism; one who was born and bred in the state of Indiana and the other who referred to Kentucky bluegrass as home; one who taught more comfortably with traditional desks in a row and the other who would scrap those desks for a Harkness table (oval table that fosters discussion with minimum teacher intervention). Nonetheless, Harry D. Frick and Bradford W. Trevathan were far more similar than dissimilar, and I found each an intriguing study, not in contrast but in common. The connective tissue that bonded the two as one could best be explained by their type A personalities. All pertinent links emanated from this behavioral orientation. I gleaned that brevity was the key to engagement with each of these men. From devouring a quick lunch to corresponding with perfunctory emails and rapidly scurrying on campus, I appreciated their haste in completing tasks. I too soon attempted to imitate them— without much success, I might add.

I first became acquainted with Harry upon his arrival at Culver in 1985 when he joined the History Department and assisted coaching the CMA basketball team. In both arenas, I found Harry's knowledge of and appreciation for history and basketball to be superlative. Harry candidly admitted that his devotion to serious study of history came well after his collegiate years. I suspect that we know many people who came to appreciate learning later in life, and Harry's admission apparently confirmed this time delay for himself. Better later than never, one would counter, and Culver profited as a result.

During one summer day in 1990, while working toward my master of arts degree in Russian language at Indiana University in Bloomington, I was approached on IU's campus by a stranger. He knew my name and that I worked at Culver. Initially confounded, I wondered how this person could know about me. I would not suggest that I felt the Russian mafia or a KGB agent was tracking my every movement. That embellishment would detract from my first encounter with Brad. He had read an article, with accompanying photographs, in the Culver Alumni Magazine of my previous spring's trip to the Soviet Union. To recognize someone walking across Indiana University's campus from a photograph astonished me. It's not as if I were a noted political figure or entertainment celebrity. Brad, who was in the process of applying for a position at Culver, possessed an astounding memory, and this ubiquitous trait served him well at Culver. Yes, he got the job, and Culver profited as a result.

Harry, for all intents and purposes, was a basketball aficionado all his life. Growing up in the state of Indiana, this would come as no great surprise. Make no mistake that Harry was no Jimmy Chitwood from the movie *Hoosiers* fame, but he knew the game, played the game in his hometown of Monticello, and could coach the game—all very well. He and I assisted Head Coach Bill Hart, and Harry instantly infused detailed preparation and organization into the program. I recall numerous players who could impersonate Harry instructing tip drills during practice, and their affectionate mocking of him became a sign of their respect for his coaching abilities. Harry and I shared many humorous encounters during our seasons of coaching together, from scouting visiting teams on our schedule to visiting a former area high school player who was in the Marshall County jail. From local county officials at the bi-county and sectional tournaments to coaching adversaries, I learned that Harry D. Frick was both well-known and respected as a basketball authority in the northern parts of the state. His previous head coaching stints at Wabash and Triton, as well as the numerous clinics he held, garnered him such a well-earned reputation. In the 1990s, Harry took the reins of CMA basketball and later of CGA basketball. In both instances, he led his teams to highly successful seasons before eventually relinquishing his coaching whistle once and for all to pursue more academic endeavors that would enrich and strengthen the Academies. A demonstration of the basketball historian within Harry is an acknowledgment that he started researching, interviewing key figures, and writing articles for the *Indiana Basketball History* magazine. He chronicled games, seasons, and legends of the high school game in the Hoosier State, and his published pieces have announced the name of Harry D. Frick IV, as one quite familiar with the lure and the lore of basketball throughout the state.

Brad's extracurricular contribution to Culver was best promulgated within the speech team. Coaching with colleagues Mitch Barnes and Dr. Jacquie Erwin, Brad's penchant for the gift of rhetoric was unmistakable, and his tutelage of student competitors proved invaluable for so many of them. Culver gained greater statewide recognition for the team's participation in tournaments throughout the state, and this translated to success at the highest levels. Brad's memory of student performances from the arenas that he coached (usually interpretative prose, poetry, drama, and humor) was remarkable. I would venture to suggest that Brad was able to recall nearly every student who worked tirelessly with him in preparation for major competitions. I am reminded of our first encounter in Bloomington, where his ability to recall illustrated one of his most prominent attributes. Not overtly familiar with techniques and strategies for effective speech competitions, I suspect that an ability to recall information quickly and then to articulate a response essentially provides an advantage to those who possess such a capacity. Brad Trevathan remained precisely that sort of individual, and undoubtedly, he imparted this ability to his competing students.

Harry, ever the dapper, dashing, tall, lanky fellow, struck quite an imposing figure on campus, if for no other reason than for his impeccable attire. I am not certain who was his haberdasher, but clearly, Harry spent considerable time and money (by his own confession) on his clothing selection. Some of those flamingo, pink trousers or frogged, Kelly-green ones were eye-popping, but Harry would rarely be seen without a formal dress shirt and tailored blazer. This attention to detail transferred to the endeavors he undertook to broaden the department and campus curriculum. Harry, one of the most voracious readers I ever met, studied extensively about the Vietnam War. In fact, he visited Vietnam to gain greater perspective of the decades-long combat in Southeast Asia. Upon his return, he initiated a new course within the History Department: the history of the Vietnam War. The course, widely popular as an upper-level elective, could easily have been included in any college course catalogue as a challenging offering to its students. Further evidence of his diligent preparation and organization would be two mammoth enterprises that he again constructed. The first, the Global Studies Institute, brought speakers with international viewpoints to campus and expanded opportunities for Culver students to engage these noted players from the world stage of politics, economics, and social orders. The second, the School for the Entrepreneur, became another Frick creation that mimicked what some of the most prestigious colleges and universities were offering. Namely, students would be able to compete with ideas for starting their own companies, and in many cases, they actually secured investors to execute their innovation plans. Harry's intentionality of thinking outside the box caught fire with several colleagues and, more notably, many students.

Brad, not one who lavished himself with the latest fashions from Tommy Hilfiger, Ralph Lauren, or Calvin Klein, instead developed other methods by which to distinguish himself as one of impeccable taste. His expertise for baking delectable desserts endeared him to his peers and his students. From his heavenly mint chocolate chip brownies to his world-class macaroons, Brad's assiduous attention to pleasuring our palates became as significant as his involvement and leadership in supplemental organizations on campus. Working in the college advising office, under the tutelage of Dr. O'Neal Turner, afforded Brad multiple opportunities to learn about colleges and universities throughout the country. By visiting both elite and not-so-elite institutions of higher learning, researching the college selection and admittance process, and guiding students through the essay writing portions of the application, Brad became one of the most crucial of personnel for juniors and seniors (second and first classmen). I recall referring many of my students with questions about college directly to Brad; I do not ever recall any of them returning to me with unanswered questions. Two other groups that drew Brad's attention and his active participation were the "no-labels group" and the multicultural awareness retreat. Both of these constituent endeavors focused upon diversity awareness and guidance, and Brad's intentional support proved invaluable to students, seeking their own acceptance as well as to those students who sought support for their friends and classmates. In many ways, Bradford Trevathan became the beacon of light that shined brightly upon diversity, tolerance, and acceptance.

Type A personalities often indicate that these are people who find time very valuable. People might be described as motivated; they might be described as impatient; they might be described as both motivated and impatient. Their thoughts are often focused upon concrete ideas or matters at hand. Such "textbook" analysis appears underwhelming at best; rather, only when these traits are applicable to those we call colleagues and friends do these become relevant. Harry D. Frick IV and Bradford W. Trevathan, residents in the same apartment building and across the hall from one another, charter members of the McGovern group of like-minded progressives, reading appetites quenched only by further reading, masters of Andy of Mayberry and MASH trivia, addicted to epic movies, and colleagues who shared a mutual admiration and respect for one another, have had their names carved on more than

Culver benches adorning the campus. They are etched on the hearts and minds of countless students and fellow instructors. I was merely one of those most fortunate who came face-to-face with these type A's, and consequently, I came to appreciate the value of time, a bit more than I ever had, thanks largely to Harry and Brad!

Culver Daughters, Sing Thy Praise

Lest one thinks that this chapter is reserved solely for the graduates of Culver Girls Academy, I suggest that these women, through their service to and love for the Academies, are Culver legends as much as their male counterparts. Each of them, in their own distinctive style and praiseworthy achievements, has assisted in stitching the fabric of the history and the culture of the school. Admittedly, I did not work as closely with some of these women, but I recognize that they have been instrumental in leadership, in collaboration, in support, in innovation, and in creativity that propelled Culver to heights not envisaged with its inception in 1894. The following is my brief and humble shoutout to each of these remarkable individuals who have made Culver more vibrant, more enlightened, and more noteworthy. Indeed, they are legendary daughters of Culver.

Mary Frances England: One could not begin to recount the story of Culver Girls Academy without highlighting the career of the very woman whose foresight and fortitude in founding the school establish her as "she, who is without peer." My interactions with Mai-Fan were limited, but my vantage point never wavered from applauding her tenacity, her refinement, and her prudence. The pillars upon which the foundation of the school was laid are unmistakably etched upon the broad shoulders of this giant of a woman. Her composition of the CGA "Baccalaureate Hymn" (one of the most beautiful of all Culver music) underscored her talent and passion for both CGA and the young women who would eventually glide through the arch on graduation day.

CGA Baccalaureate Hymn

(Last Lines)
Source of wisdom, Thee we praise
Now hear our plea and humble call
Embrace Thy Culver daughters all
Make us ever fair and strong
Free from ills of want and wrong
Keep us true in all Thy ways
Culver daughters sing Thy praise
For all our youth and yesterdays. (Culver Academies)

Julie Thornburg: By all accounts, Julie, a native Hoosier, became the first female instructor at Culver, beginning her long-standing, illustrious career of teaching Spanish in 1976 before exiting Culver in 2017. Hundreds of my history and government students in that time span were also instructed by Mrs. Thornburg, and those same students echoed sentiments of appreciation and praise for the demanding expectations that were imposed within their Spanish classes. All of them may have not become bilingually proficient, but they learned from a master that diligence and preparation were keys to successful foreign language learning. I appreciated greatly Julie's collegiality, especially when I served as a Russian instructor within the department. However, one of my most cherished memories of our times together involved riding our bicycles weekly around Lake Maxinkuckee after a day of classroom teaching. Fittingly, or perhaps not so much so, we undid that ten-mile ride by stopping at Mr. T's Drugstore for chocolate sodas before reaching campus. Somehow, and not so surprisingly, we did not become "poster material" for physical fitness, but our conversations throughout those rides solidified our friendship for more than three decades.

Carolyn Kline: Wearer of many hats during her distinguished career at the Academies, Carolyn Kline best reflected both diversity and expertise in the varied roles she occupied. Perhaps better than anyone I came to know, Carolyn recognized that boarding school life required active participation in both the residential life and academic arenas. Her roles as a CGA counselor and dean of girls supplemented her primary love as an English language and literature instructor, which culminated in Carolyn's promotion as department chair of English. She deftly transitioned from dormitory to classroom life, all the while building budding relationships with students and colleagues across the campus. Carolyn and I became well-acquainted with one another during our stints as department chairs, and this alliance solidified when the English Department and the History Department merged to form the Humanities Department. The fact that the two of us are like-minded political creatures only has intensified our admiration and esteem for one another. I would add that being able to work with two of her grandchildren, Maeve and Frank Kline, in the advanced placement government and politics courses, affirmed the importance of reading as a lifelong endeavor. Unquestionably, their grandmother's influence paid and continues to pay dividends in their lives. To borrow from English literature, Carolyn Kline is a "woman for all seasons." Avid reader, creative seamstress, and world-class chef aptly could describe Mrs. Kline. I am honored to append this list by one: cherished friend.

Joan Bess: As one of the head librarians for the Academies, Joan brought to her daily tasks a genteel spirit that infected her staff, making the Huffington Library one of the most desirable venues on campus. The conducive atmosphere for study and research was enhanced by the warm, engaging, and accommodating dispositions of those who worked within the walls of the Huff, to which it so affectionately was referred. Joan's quiet but effective leadership was most discernible to all those who sought refuge from the onslaught of the busyness of the school. As a matter of fact, I suspect that many of my History and Humanities Department colleagues actually took up residence in the library. During the day-long move from the Memorial Legion Building to the new headquarters in the Huffington Library in the spring of 1993, Joan's organizational and leadership skills were put to the ultimate test. She and her staff passed with flying colors. Every student and adult completed the laborious task of moving books from the old location to the new digs. What a delightful way to spend a day off from classes! Joan's love for Culver was further witnessed whenever she patronized the numerous athletic competitions on campus. Quite naturally, as the devoted wife to Larry, Culver's widely popular athletic director, and as the supportive mother to Julie, Larry Jr., Ginny, and Angie, Joan's presence may have remained in the shadows, but that attendance was always heartfelt. Leadership is best learned when those who follow do so without hesitation, without fear, and without affirmation. Joan Bess, as a Culver giant, evoked such qualities within the rest of us.

Jacquie Erwin: Wearer of sassy hats, dangling jewelry, and an effervescent smile, Dr. Erwin cast a presence far and wide across the entire campus. Her towering impact will be felt for generations, long after she leaves behind the generated vocabulary lists her students came to loathe yet simultaneously appreciate. "Dr. Evil," the affectionate moniker bestowed upon by students in Jacquie's classes, first and foremost relished classroom time with her charges. Always "on stage, and on cue," the teacher in her soul would never allow a moment to elapse without challenging her classes to think creatively, read prodigiously, and write cogently. She epitomized the essence of dynamic English instruction, and I doubt that I could recall who may have garnered more success at her craft than Jacquie.

She and I collaborated as cochairs of the Humanities Department, and I was grateful beyond words for the wisdom and graciousness she shared with all of our colleagues. She commanded respect from student and faculty alike by and through her industrious work ethic and creative talent. Perhaps no one more than Jacquie best exemplified what it meant to teach, and subsequently lead, by example. Her commitment to educating the whole individual (body, mind, spirit) could be felt by her presence throughout the many quarters of campus life. Adorning her Sunday finery to attend chapel services, traversing the highways throughout the Midwest to coach the speech team, supporting CMA and CGA at spring and autumn parades, hosting social events from department Christmas parties to the class of 1969 reunions (her late husband, Lew, was a proud member of the class of 1969), baker extraordinaire of delectable treats for mentees and fellow colleagues, and yes, always and forever an exemplar by putting others before herself. I stood in awe of her boundless energy, positive reinforcement, and collaborative spirit. Jacquie Erwin loved Culver; perhaps more fitting is that Culver loved her!

Kathy Lintner: How does one follow in the footsteps of a Culver legend whose persona seemed larger than life itself? Such was the narrative for Kathy Lintner, who eventually assumed the roles of dean of the Academies and principal following the death of Alexander Nagy. I never conversed with Kathy about the transition to such a lofty administrative position, but I could not help but wonder that she must have experienced some awkward moments and even challenges from various Culver constituents to her newly acquired roles. Kathy's career at Culver, interrupted by a brief stint of teaching at Knox Community High School, included teaching within the English Department and Humanities Department as well as working in the Head of School's office. Her avocation of teaching courses in myth and literature, frequently team taught with her trusted friend and colleague, Dr. Richard Davies, certainly allowed her intimate interaction with students. This particular senior elective course became one of the most popular with students, and Kathy's passion for this genre largely was responsible for its appeal.

Although the *Star Wars* phenomenon had little appeal for me, Kathy and I cultivated an interest in the fascination with James Dean, the movie icon from Fairmount, Indiana. We made the trek to his hometown, toured the Dean Galleria Museum, visited his high school where he first performed in a play, and even paid our respects at his gravesite. This blast from the past venture was one of my most memorable of Culver experiences, and I was honored to be able to share this with Kathy. I felt quite inadequate to comprehend the many responsibilities that Kathy undertook in her position as dean of the Academies, but I came to realize that she took great pride in collaborating with Kevin MacNeil in leading Culver into the twenty-first century with personnel and curricular reform.

I would be gravely mistaken to believe that I could record comprehensively both the challenges and accomplishments that Kathy Lintner incurred during her Culver career. However, allow me to suggest that the Lintner imprint upon the Academies indelibly has been cemented in its history.

Cathy Duke: An elegant dancer, a whimsical spirit, a refined lady, and a dynamic instructor aptly describe this 1970 CGA graduate. Cathy returned to her alma mater to elevate Culver to elevations that even the most graceful of ballerinas, thrust into the air, could not have envisioned. Daughter of Chan and Dorry Mitzell, longtime Culver employees, Cathy distinguished herself as a consummate, lifelong learner. I came to know and appreciate her first by observation of the many performances she directed and second through serving together as department chairs of our respective disciplines. Dance vision productions became yearly highlights of the Fine Arts Department for the benefit of the entire school and the surrounding communities.

Having taught several of these sprightly young ladies, I came to understand better the amount of effort that they and Mrs. Duke exerted to stage such entertaining shows. The dance for athletes class, which invariably brought together some of the most muscular males on campus, illustrated the variety, complexity, and innovation that captured the fascination of so many of us. Toward the end of my tenure at Culver, I chose to view numerous classes in disciplines quite removed from my own. One such visit was Cathy's introductory dance class. I marveled at the structure and discipline that she inculcated into the lesson while still evoking utter enjoyment on the part of her dancing proteges. This was one of the most intriguing and pleasant experiences I encountered when observing other colleagues *take center stage.* Cathy's engaging demeanor, perceptive insights, and collegial spirit became most discernible to me when we met together within our department chair sessions, and I grew accustomed to listening to her commentary with attentive ears. Much like the dancer whose feet will not rest, Cathy, as one of the original daughters of Culver, is lauded for her commitment to the perpetual growth of the Academies.

Emily Uebler: Mrs. Uebler was one of my finest hires, bar none! Emily joined Culver with her husband, J. D., in 2010. From her first day, she established herself as a master of her discipline, widely popular with her students, and competitor with Dr. Erwin for smartest-dressed instructor. I stood in awe of Emily as she pursued advanced studies for her doctorate while simultaneously preparing stimulating and challenging courses for her students in humanities. Her diligence, conscientiousness, and professionalism garnered her the respect and admiration of her students and colleagues, and consequently, naming her as director of the Writing Center became a logical path for her promotion. This expansion of her responsibilities was noteworthy because the Writing Center spanned beyond the Humanities Department to include disciplines across the campus. Again, Emily's attention to detail and organizational skills drew the praise and confidence of all who worked closely with her. One could not possibly neglect her cheerful and courteous demeanor. I, for one, became infected by her positive and caring approach to living. Her generosity and thoughtfulness in providing delectable treats (her lemon and lime bars were worthy of serving to royalty) and luncheons on a regular basis endeared her to every single department member. I recall informing her that she could easily have opened her own culinary shop and put several others in town out of business. In fact, many of her own students asked if she would bake their graduation cakes for them. All of this, of course, was not what made Emily Uebler a giant among the daughters of Culver. However, it certainly did not hurt her cause either!

Anne Duff: Where would Culver have been had it not experienced a wee bit of Scotland in its midst? Anne's picturesque scenes of daily living reminded us of the cosmopolitan view that she and husband, Charles, brought to Culver. Unquestionably, their artistic talents strengthened our Fine Arts Department, and as such, so did the accomplished works of their students. Anne exuded charm, wit, and a critical eye for examination of all things Culver. As department chair, member of multiple evaluation committees, and artist extraordinaire, Anne's forte was her resolute commitment to excellence. Her quiet yet perceptive nature allowed her to impact decision-making at various levels. The fact that the Fine Arts Department was housed in multiple quarters on campus necessitated that Anne exerted considerable effort to be involved visibly and actively from music to drama to visual arts. I once remarked that she needed roller skates to traverse from one end of the campus to another. She demurely smiled and suggested that no task was too great for a determined Scottish gal. She possessed both grit and enchantment, and the impact of her tenacity and artistic flair would be felt by many of us who came to love and appreciate her. I especially enjoyed the fascinating stories she wove of growing up near the Scottish-English border. Most assuredly, her grown children, Tim, Susanna, and Jeremy, would concur that their mother, Anne Duff, was deserving of both Scottish and Culver fame.

Lynn Rasch: Sister Rasch, as I would come to know her (because of her support for Latter-day Saints students) remarkably etched her name in Culver lore. I had been unaware, prior to my final year at Culver, of the spiritual development that she fostered with Culver's Latter-day Saints students. Driving them often to a sacrament meeting in Plymouth and serving as a campus support system for those same students underscored Sister Rasch's personal spirituality. Dean Rasch distinguished herself first as a CGA graduate of 1976 and later as dean of Culver Girls Academy; however, all those years between these two circumstances prepared and propelled Lynn to ascend the ladder of Culver greatness. Dean Rasch, like several other notable giants in Culver lore, wore many hats in her service to her alma mater. Her involvement with the Horsemanship Department as instructor and chaperone for Presidential Inaugural Parade events revealed the affinity she held for this equine discipline. Her invaluable labors as CGA counselor, assistant dean of girls and dean of girls underscored the significance of aiding young ladies in residential life and leadership opportunities. Lynn, first and foremost, brought compassion and keen perception to her responsibilities. I readily observed these qualities while serving on disciplinary committee hearings with her. Always professional and approachable, Lynn Rasch's cordial nature served as an archetype for Culver Girls Academy. Ever concerned with the welfare of Culver students, she consciously made each decision with that in mind. The Academies were beyond blessed that this daughter returned home to lead future daughters of the school.

Jennifer Cerny: In the spring of 2000, I interviewed an intern candidate from Ypsilanti, Michigan, who was transparently overqualified to become an intern. Within minutes of that conversation and hearing Jen speak of cognitive dissonance, I readily submitted her resume to our English Department chair, Carolyn Kline. This transpired as a rather prophetic "rejection" to a candidate who belonged at Culver—just not as an intern. Jen Cerny would be one of the most cerebral individuals I met at Culver. I coveted her as a budding history scholar, and when the departments of English and History merged to form Humanities, my wish for the two of us to become colleagues came to fruition. Jen's innovation and critical thinking skills imparted to her students strengthened her classroom endeavors. Whenever I had opportunities to observe her in action, I marveled at the manner in which she deliberately infused alternate ways to examine literary and historical issues. One mark of superior instruction is prompting students to examine perspectives different from the norm, and I found myself doing precisely that, along with Jen's charges. I was never fond of committee work, but if Jen were a member of that committee, I found that her perceptions and insights tempered my impatience. Jen, ever the cogent thinker, articulate speaker, and persuasive author, best replicated scholarship at the highest level, and few, if any Culver daughters, could excel her in this regard.

Nancy Nowalk McKinnis: As with so many other women whose stars illuminated brightly, Nancy's work across the campus spectrum illustrated her prominence as a giant of Culver. A St. Mary's College graduate, Nancy served as a CGA basketball coach, CGA counselor, fine arts instructor, and Leadership Department instructor. In each instance, Nancy's engaging, warm disposition attracted students to her, and consequently, she assumed the mantle of quietly affirming mentor.

Validating each student as a worthwhile contributor to a project, a course, or a larger enterprise on campus distinguished Nancy from many of her peers. Her penchant for objectivity and acceptance of others' perspectives added to her inclination of putting others first and service as a way of living. Nancy supported hundreds of senior service projects, and many students appreciated a gentle (or in a few cases, not so gentle) nudge from her in completing their self-directed service endeavors. I had the privilege of instructing two of her children, Robert and Margaret, and both of them exuded the same quiet charm and perseverance in meeting the American government course expectations. When compiling records of countless Culver employees, Nancy's fame will not be a result of self-promotion. Just the opposite will be the case, as she gently but effectively directed Culver to seek of itself how best to serve others.

Catherine Saxon Battersby: If Culver ever experienced someone whose background in classics was robust, it undoubtedly would be Catherine. Mrs. Battersby's extensive training in classical languages, history, and culture illustrated that she was supremely competent in both the Humanities Department and Foreign Language Department. In fact, in 2001, she began her teaching career at Culver by instructing languages. Latin and Greek would be the springboard to her transition to teaching with the rest of us in the enlarged House of Clio, now that the History Department had been broadened to the Humanities Department. Catherine's penchant for the classical world of ancient Rome and Greece became a citadel for advanced instruction in advanced placement European history. She transformed this lightly enrolled course into one of the most highly sought after by talented seniors during her time within the department. Perhaps even more noteworthy is the relationship that she cultivated with the Spoleto Institute in Italy for both instructors and students, aspiring to study classical culture in Italy during summer terms. The footprints that she left upon this collaborative enterprise were as if she herself were wearing the boot of Italy. Students and instructors from the disciplines of humanities, foreign languages, and fine arts actively sought Catherine as the liaison to Spoleto and other geographic regions of Italy. Additionally, Catherine mentored the authorship of the student-run publications, *The Gazette* and *The Quill*. Under the watchful and discerning eye of Catherine, the students' articles and artwork were sometimes provocative, sometimes informative, and sometimes whimsical. Whatever aspect these pieces conveyed, they prompted the reader to think critically about the intended message. Catherine, with her husband, Richard, retreated to England in retirement, but the hallmark of Catherine Saxon Battersby's greatness was left upon the shores of Lake Max and many ports beyond.

Emily Payson Ryman: If for no other reason, this Michigan State Spartan is deserving of high accolades. Rumor had it that Emily bleeds green and white. In all seriousness, this Michigan native possessed long and storied ties to the history of the school. Emily is the proud granddaughter of Edward Payson, who came to Culver on a bugle scholarship and graduated from CMA in 1922. He returned to Culver to teach music and served as the band director until retirement in 1967. Emily's grandmother Dorothy Eisenhard Payson was the daughter of George Eisenhard, who founded the science wing at Culver. As a history buff, I found it fascinating that I would come to know someone such as Emily who actually could be considered a genuine legacy of Culver.

That said, Emily's preeminent contributions and service to the school mimicked those of her grandfather. I first met Emily when she served as a CGA counselor for Argonne Tower in 1982, and her gentle and caring demeanor affirmed that she was seriously cognizant of her role of "in loco parentis." Over the years, and as Emily undertook further responsibilities within the summer school office and winter school admissions department, that same attention to serving our students magnified. The kindheartedness that I first witnessed within Emily in 1982 never softened. Emily placed the health, safety, and welfare of all Culver students, winter and summer schools, to be of utmost importance. Perhaps better than most, Emily understood what life away from home was like for Culver students. Most assuredly, Grandfather and Grandmother Payson were proud of their granddaughter for carrying forth their legacy of Culver allegiance. She truly is a Culver daughter whose praise I sing.

The Twenty-Five

One of the innovative changes to occur during my tenure at Culver included the formation of the faculty intern program (name more recently altered as faculty mentors) begun under the auspices of Dean Ralph Manuel, head of school, and Dean Alexander Nagy, principal of the Academies, in the 1984–85 academic year. Initially, six bright, young men arrived at Culver, fresh from completing their undergraduate degrees. Due to the success of that first year, the program was expanded in subsequent years to roughly a dozen college graduates, to include both men and women. These eager, wide-eyed, aspiring educators would spend a year honing their skills in the classroom under the tutelage of a master instructor, assist with various athletic and extracurricular activities to gain expertise in the coaching realms, and work closely with residential life counselors in helping supervise the barracks of Culver Military Academy and the dormitories of Culver Girls Academy. These responsibilities became known as "triple-threat" challenges that would prepare the interns for future employment in private boarding schools.

What was unique about this one-year experience is that it would provide the recent college graduates with experiences that would help them decide if education in this sort of environment was for them. Many of these interns would decide that they were well-suited to continue in this professional endeavor. Some, in fact, remained at Culver when vacancies became available in their chosen disciplines. Many found employment at other institutions, private and public, throughout the country. Some would discover that this year of boarding school life was of benefit, but they chose to pursue advanced degrees in law schools, med schools, and business schools. Some found greater ventures awaiting them by joining an organization such as the Peace Corps or working in a family-owned business. No matter the direction that these young men and women followed, Culver benefited tremendously from their invaluable contributions that they provided to the Academies. I suspect that most, if not all, the interns would agree that they too profited from their year at this school, nestled "behind the corn silk curtain" of Indiana, as the illustrious Dean Nagy would characterize Culver. In my thirty-four years as a "Culver man," I was fortunate and blessed to have worked with twenty-five faculty interns. The following is merely a modest summary of those men and women who impacted the entire Culver campus by their presence and their active participation. I wish to pay tribute to each of them. A testament to this assertion is the fact that I can still recall their birthdays, alma maters, and years of service during their intern year. Well, at least I boast that I can still recall this information. Time will tell if advanced years of retirement allow me to continue to do so. With all due respect and humility, here is my clumsy but sincere attempt to recognize each of them.

Patrick McHugh, Franklin and Marshall College, Lancaster, Pennsylvania, 1985–86

Working with Patrick, my first intern, proved to be one of the most rewarding and memorable experiences of my life. Initially, the responsibility given to me to provide counsel to this fellow overwhelmed me. However, after just a few days, I knew that the two of us would become far more than mentor/mentee. We developed a collegial relationship that advanced to becoming lifelong friends. In fact, I visited Patrick in 1988 when he taught and coached at Friends Central School in Philadelphia, and I was honored to attend his wedding in Agawam, Massachusetts, in 1993. Patrick tirelessly worked at crafting American history lessons for his students. His knowledge of our nation's past was quite strong, as was his command of writing. I learned from him that Franklin and Marshall College required history majors to complete a writing workshop that enabled them to communicate effectively. This would prove to be useful to Patrick as he waded through the myriad of essays that awaited him in his American history classes. Patrick's avocation of running prepared him to serve as an assistant coach for both cross-country and track. He and Coach Mike Chastain have maintained a close connection to this very day. Patrick did not bring a car with him to Culver, so I happily aided him wherever he needed to venture. I recall driving him to some distance races that he entered and pridefully watched him excel. I never thought that Patrick had the physique of a runner, but he ran like the wind whenever I observed him. I encouraged Patrick to help me coach basketball for Culver's junior varsity boys' team during the winter months. He reluctantly consented, and one of the more humorous moments occurred when, following a time-out, he sent only four players back on the floor. I couldn't understand why our team was having difficulty guarding the opposition until someone on the bench brought it unceremoniously to our attention. Patrick lost interest in coaching basketball after this episode. I cannot fathom why!

The friendship bonds established throughout the school year became even stronger when we visited Chicago for a weekend and hit some of the bars, normally reserved for the younger college crowd. I was out of my element, but I was undeterred from having fun with my friend. It is rather ironic today to realize that Patrick, a born and bred East Coast boy from Baltimore who struggled a bit with Midwestern rural American life, took up residence with his wife and two sons in the Windy City. He later claimed that Chicago possessed all the charm that he once felt the Midwest lacked.

Before the school year closed its doors, we celebrated our birthdays, separated by just one day, in late May. The lump in my throat and tears in my eyes could not conceal how much I was going to miss my first intern when we embraced one final time. For numerous years, Patrick McHugh would remain the measuring stick by which I gauged all interns.

Alan Loehr, Tulane University, New Orleans, Louisiana, 1986–87

Technically, Alan Loehr served as an intern with Dean Alexander Nagy. However, due to some circumstances that prevented Alan from gaining considerable teaching experience in the classroom setting, Alan worked with me, teaching Western civilization to Culver freshmen. Never would I meet someone with greater humility than when I met this native Floridian who made his way to north-central Indiana. Alan had a tenuous connection to Culver in that he was a fraternity brother to one of Dean Ralph Manuel's sons at Tulane. That chain link that was first established in 1986 has been forged by iron as Alan presently serves as the Culver alumni director in a role unsurpassed by anyone who previously served in our development and alumni offices.

I cannot state with more clarity when I write that unquestionably Alan Loehr is one of the giants in Culver's celebrated history. He is a Culver man in every sense of that reputable title, and I am certain that the Culver legion of alumni would underscore this acclamation. I knew immediately that Alan had a penchant for detail. He could rattle off the nicknames or mascots for almost every college or university within the country. He informed me that being a connoisseur of ESPN allowed him to acquire such knowledge. I believe that sort of mastery of trivia has helped him in his role as alumni director. Alan has worked laboriously to learn about Culver and its legions of alums. No detail is too minute for Alan to record mentally in preparation for not only alumni weekends at Culver but for his day-to-day contact with these same people. His knowledge of the men and women who have walked the paths of the campus is truly masterful. I suspect that Alan would give credit to other Culver giants who served before and with him in a wide array of capacities. However, what distinguishes Alan Loehr from many of these other legends of Culver is that he has surpassed them in character, in leadership, in modesty, and in stature.

In many ways it was as if the position of alumni director was created specifically for him. Prior to his ascension within the alumni office, however, Alan gained footing within the classroom. One of the most memorable occasions I recall is Alan, impeccably attired as if modeling for *GQ* magazine, paced in front of the freshmen Western civilization students in his stocking feet. It is more apt to say that he glided rather than paced at the forefront of the class. I was taken aback slightly, but when I inquired about "teaching shoeless" after the conclusion of the class, he simply stated that he did not want to fall "flat on his ass" in front of the students. His neatly polished leather penny loafers would never maneuver the slick tile floors within the History Department classroom in the old Legion Memorial Building. His reasoning being quite sound nonetheless caused me to chuckle. I assured Alan that he was an excellent classroom instructor; however, he concluded by year's end that the classroom setting was not one of his strengths. I suspect that his own humble nature revealed that his expectations for himself were lofty enough to causes him to look to other venues for his contribution to life at Culver. The History Department's loss became the alumni office's gain, and Culver could not have been more grateful.

I came to admire and hold in the highest esteem this Tulane graduate. Our mutual interest in tennis provided for numerous conversations about the game familiar to most at Wimbledon. Alan's coaching expertise and penchant for working with young people helped to keep Culver at the forefront of tennis dominance in the state of Indiana. From the most skilled Latin American player who could hit with topspin to the neophyte looking to find his niche on the courts, Alan wasted no time in offering his guidance and assistance. Alan and I cemented our friendship in a variety of ways, but most poignant for me is the excursion to England in November 1994, a month following the untimely death of Dean Alexander Nagy. Alan and his wife, Wendy, the director of admissions, Rich Edwards, and I traveled together for several days. Sampling British public transport, plays, and pubs confirmed my belief that in the midst of mourning our academic dean, I was witnessing the setting sun becoming a rising one. The torch was passed, and Alan was just the person to carry that flame to its new destination: the dawning of a new Culver era.

Ed McBride, Franklin and Marshall College, Lancaster, Pennsylvania, 1987–88

Much like Alan Loehr, Ed McBride was not assigned to work directly with me as a faculty intern. His mentor, Michael Bouton, a fellow American history instructor, became gravely ill during this academic year, and I offered my assistance to Ed as mentor and friend. So here we have another "Dip" as in Franklin and Marshall Diplomats with whom I could become acquainted and work. Ed, another East Coaster, hailing from New Jersey, came just as prepared in his knowledge and appreciation for American history and expository writing as Patrick McHugh had been two years earlier. I recall telling myself that I must take a visit to Franklin and Marshall College to learn more about its collegiate offerings, particularly its Writing Laboratory.

In many ways, I felt both empathy and praise for Ed. His industrious work ethic and conscientious attitude toward his intern responsibilities were laudatory. Michael Bouton, the assigned master instructor for Ed, was so grievously ill (he would eventually succumb to cancer after the school year) that Ed frequently flew solo in the classroom. Teaching in an adjoining classroom to Ed did provide me an opportunity to observe and offer assistance. That said, Ed really entered his intern year quite polished, and he required little guidance from me. Most of our conversations involved lessons of our nation's history and fascinating anecdotal information on characters that shaped our nation, both overtly and from behind the scenes. I recall that Ed's passion for military and political history inspired most of his discussions in the classroom.

Further ties to Mr. McBride could be found on the tennis court. He and I both enjoyed the sport and the history behind the game, and we engaged in tennis battles, usually which found him on the winning side of the court. His coaching prowess actually was quite varied as he also assisted the soccer and wrestling programs. He understood well the nature of boarding school life and the necessity of staying involved in as many activities as possible.

As the school year approached its closing, I was pleased and honored to write reference letters for Ed as he searched for employment in private secondary education. I knew both cerebrally and viscerally that he would strengthen any school's faculty. Regretfully, we had no vacancy within the History Department for the following academic year, or I am quite certain that we would have offered employment to Ed. Nevertheless, Ed did land a position with the Asheville School in North Carolina, and he distinguished himself as both a gentleman and scholar in the Tar Heel State.

Scot Mellor, College of Wooster, Wooster, Ohio, 1988–89

Hailing from the Buckeye State (Killbuck), I received my first faculty intern with roots firmly planted in the Midwest. Scot Mellor, much like Patrick McHugh, was an avid runner, and as such, he worked with Coach Michael Chastain in both cross-country and track. Additionally, like Patrick, I believe that Coach Chastain and Scot have remained in contact at coaching clinics since Scot remained in the Hoosier State following his intern year at Culver by securing a position in Indianapolis.

What I recollect most about this year with Scot were discussions about the summer Olympic Games that occurred in Seoul, South Korea, in the autumn of 1988. The passion for following the track and field events prompted much excitement for Scot, and although I enjoyed watching these games, I deferred to my friend and colleague, Mike Chastain, to engage Scot on the complexities of the individual events. I could make references to Soviet versus American track competitions during the Cold War era, but that would be the extent of my track and field knowledge. Does anyone else still recall Ralph Boston or Valery Brumel? I am certain that Mike and Scot do. Scot's initial reticence in the classroom was more a result of his quiet nature. He was a gentle and kind soul, and I remember him as empathetic toward his students and athletes. I found that he related quite well to those reserved students who sought affirmation before engaging with a classroom discussion. In many ways Scot brought to mind my own high school experiences as I too was one of those introverted students, often too timid to assume leadership roles. I think that I would have profited from having Scot as one of my own instructors.

Jeff Kellmanson, Franklin and Marshall College, Lancaster, Pennsylvania, 1989–90

Wow! Another Diplomat from F&M, and another East Coaster, this one hailing from Upstate New York (Pittsford)! Just as Patrick McHugh and Ed McBride before him, Jeff's background in history and his command of expository writing were superlative. For certain, I must visit this college in the heart of Pennsylvania Amish country!

Jeff's engaging personality and love for basketball (he was a die-hard Syracuse University fan) made for easy rapport between the two of us. I guess it was not all that unusual that he loved the Orange and Jim Boeheim since his roots were planted in the northern stretches of the Empire State. Jeff transferred his love of basketball to assisting the boys' basketball program at Culver. I was no longer involved directly with CMA basketball, but I followed Jeff and his team as they experienced firsthand Hoosier hysteria in the smallest of rural communities surrounding Culver. Jeff's love for history and global affairs proved invaluable to me as he enthusiastically aided me when I brought to Culver graduate students from the University of Notre Dame who were involved with the Peace Institute, an initiative the Reverend Theodore Hesburgh, president emeritus of Notre Dame, began. Roughly a half dozen graduate students from various parts of the world answered questions from the student body about the nature of peace and obstacles confronting nations attempting to secure their own sovereignty. I had hoped to entice Jeff to accompany me during our spring break to the former USSR, and although his interest was high, he was unable to do so. However, during the planning and preparation of this venture for most of my Russian history students, I relied upon Jeff to carry the load in teaching several of the classes that we shared. His professionalism and courtesy earmarked him as one of the most dependable interns with whom I had the privilege of working.

Mike Nekritz, Northwestern University, Evanston, Illinois, 1990–91

A Big Ten Conference intern and another young man from the Midwest! Actually, Mike, born and bred in the Chicago suburbs, exuded all the panache of a Windy City resident. I loved Mike's assertiveness and confidence when he approached his tasks and challenges confronting interns. Mike combined his two passions for history and basketball in much the same fashion. He aggressively worked to prepare himself in the classroom and on the court, and he expected that his students and players would follow suit. Sometimes the students and players did not bring their "A" game, but they retained Mike's persistence that they should did not diminish his expectations for them or for him. As a talented basketball player in high school, Mike could hold his own against any of the Culver varsity players. Truth be known, he would outperform them in practice, and the good-natured trash-talking between players and Mike fostered a warm, engaging rapport among all of them.

It came as no great surprise to me that Mike would secure a position at one of the most athletically successful public high schools in the Chicago suburbs after he departed Culver. I suspect that Mike's love of basketball surpassed his love for history, but his devotion to help adolescents develop into adulthood might very well have been his greatest strength. When we parted company in June 1991, I felt quite melancholy. I did not realize how much I appreciated Mike throughout the year, and now he was departing. I am quite certain that I did not convey adequately to him what a privilege it was to work with him. I regret that still.

David Cyranoski, University of Michigan, Ann Arbor, Michigan, 1990–91

Another Big Ten university lad, and during the same year when working with Mike Nekritz, David Cyranoski's life intersected with mine in such a manner that I still feel the effects. His infectious smile, quick wit, and keen native intelligence complemented his engaging personality in the most disarming of ways. The fact that David was assigned to the Mathematics Department for his academic responsibilities speaks to his versatility because his natural inclination and college preparation would normally have led him to the History Department.

I honestly believe that Dean Nagy hired David knowing full well that numerous academic disciplines would profit from the "Cyranoski" effect. David and I shared a course in Russian and Soviet history during the second semester of the year, and his cross-pollination of disciplines proved to be a boon for those of us in the History Department. His preparation for classroom presentations was truly remarkable, and I suggested on more than one occasion that he rose to such heights despite his "mediocre" college background from Wolverine country. To be sure, he would retort that without the University of Michigan, the Big Ten Conference would be second rate academically and athletically. I would not want to admit this publicly, and especially to Spartan nation, but I connected with David, the Wolverine, in a manner that left me wondering what life might have been like had we been contemporaries on the Ann Arbor or East Lansing campuses. He brought forth a youthful spirit and invigoration within me that had long been lacking. I am not certain if either of us would have been a type of fraternity brother, but I could envision us as familial older and younger brothers. David's versatility in coaching both football and tennis solidified his well-roundedness, but I marveled more that David distinguished himself as a scholar, diverting his attention to international endeavors. After waitering in one of those yuppie pubs in his native Chicago (he actually called the suburb of Aurora home), eventually he landed in Japan, exploring further global pathways.

I found myself lamenting the fact that David and I lost contact with one another after his year at Culver. His Renaissance spirit remained with those he left behind, most notably me.

Rich Stearns, Northwestern University, Evanston, Illinois, 1991–92

A native of the Keystone State, Rich Stearns arrived at Culver after completing his bachelor's degree in history from Northwestern University. Hence, I was definitely getting my fair share of interns whose alma maters were from the Big Ten. Like Mike Nekritz and David Cyranoski before him, Rich brought with him a profound understanding of American history and a desire to share it with his students. His good-natured disposition, clever sense of humor, and quick retorts instantly served as assets he would capitalize upon in working with students and colleagues alike. I appreciated Rich as someone quite serious about teaching but equally jovial as a prankster. His collective group of interns that year kept a watchful eye on the games played upon one another. Frequently, Rich and a few other History Department interns were the masterminds of such free-spirited activities. In many ways, this particular year was a fun one because Rich and I cultivated a brotherly relationship based upon a fondness for one another. Culturally and politically, we connected, and that served as a springboard to many conversations that strengthened our respect for one another.

Rich was instrumental in helping Culver promote and develop its lacrosse program. He played the game and knew the intricacies of coaching it, so his spring season was punctuated by lacrosse tournaments throughout the Midwest. As I mentioned in the introduction to this chapter, whenever a vacancy occurred for the following year, Culver first examined the viability of hiring one of its interns from the preceding year. Such was the case for Rich Stearns. He remained at Culver for several more years as a full-time History Department member, and he continued to excel at coaching lacrosse. I was proud of his development as a first-rate instructor, and I was honored to be a small part of that progression in his career. When he departed Culver, he made his way to Seattle, where he continued to excel in private school education. Most likely, he took and continues to take that free-spiritedness with him.

John McCann, Williams College, Williamstown, Massachusetts, 1992–93

After three Jewish interns in a row (Kellmanson, Nekritz, and Stearns), I was wondering if the good dean would find me an Irish Catholic fellow.

Enter John McCann. Hailing from the Garden State of New Jersey, John matriculated to one of those prestigious "Little Ivy" schools at Williams College. From the very outset of the program in 1984–85, the male interns were long considered to have that *GQ*, preppy boy appearance, and most of them in fact did resemble that look of navy blazer, plaid tie, khaki chinos, and penny loafer shoes. John McCann was no exception, but he did bring with him a bit of the blue-collar swag of a hockey player with remnants of multiple broken noses. I soon learned the reason for such countenance: John was a former hockey player. Quite naturally CMA hockey would be ecstatic to have another coach within its domain. For the first time, I was working with an intern whose love of sport was found on the ice arena. I always assumed that the sweetest moment for hockey was when a team was "icing" the puck. OK, I realize that is a poor excuse for a pun, but that was probably my extent of knowledge of the game. John would be the one who would tell me that I should sit in the penalty box since I had taught so many hockey players over the years yet still knew little of their sport.

As it turned out, John became my most valuable intern at the most opportune time. This was the year that I first developed kidney stones (a malady that still plagues me), and it was he who would rescue me in the middle of the night to transport me to the hospital in Plymouth. When I was unable to teach for over a week, John replaced me full-time for all my classes. Upon my return to the classroom, the students groaned that they had become accustomed to John's teaching style. I did not blame them; I think that I preferred his style to mine. My Socratic method of putting the students on the spot appeared to be as antiquated as John Houseman's at Harvard Law School was in *The Paper Chase.* Nonetheless, John and I got along famously. We traveled to the Lake Michigan beaches where I once spent time as an adolescent, celebrated birthdays with a few pints of beer and whiskey chasers and talked about aspirations in life that would focus upon travel.

John met and dated a very sweet gal, Stacy, who worked in our student activities office. Eventually, the two of them married and raised five children. How ironic that they could field a basketball team, not a hockey one. I still receive yearly updates from the McCann family every Christmas, complete with photographs. I can mark the passage of time by comparing one year's photo to the next and marveling at the beautiful family that John and Stacy have. Yes, the three boys, now in their young adult years, do have that preppy look about them.

Ben Rein, Amherst College, Amherst, Massachusetts, 1993–94

Hailing from Chevy Chase, Maryland, and St. Albans Prep, another intern arrived from a "Little Ivy" college, this time Amherst, a rival to Williams College, the alma mater of John McCann. Make no mistake. Ben Rein was no hockey player. In fact, he was a star basketball player for Amherst. At least I know the rules and game of this sport, including no blue lines, no high-sticking, and no icing the puck. I was back in my element, so to speak.

Ben, a tall and striking fellow, left his imprint upon the campus in a multitude of ways. Obviously, his devotion to the game of basketball unmistakably drew fans from all corners of the campus. (Or at least from those who viewed the game invented by James Naismith as uppermost in their lives). I shall forever remember three hotshot hoopsters in one of our classes who boasted that they could take down Ben and me on the court. I conveyed to Ben that my playing days were well behind me, but he spoke with such assurance that all that was necessary was for me to lob the ball into him and he would jam it into the hoop.

For weeks in the spring of the year, much banter and trash-talking dominated our conversations. In fact, these three would-be stars (I might add "only in their dreams") drummed up such fanfare that I thought it necessary to print placards to be appropriately placed everywhere on campus, such as the dining hall, the library, the gymnasium, classroom buildings, and even the entrance grounds to the Academies. Since each of the three had honed their own nicknames of Fireman, Wolfman, and Buns, Ben and I twisted those names to suit our purposes. Hence, we exclaimed that "fireman would be extinguished, wolfman would be shaven, and buns would be tattooed," to mock these upstarts. The final result: this old man was far too old to compete, and Ben's prowess of dunking the ball was marred by incessant fouling from the three. In hindsight, we should have had a referee to monitor the violations on the court. Ben and I had a little egg on our faces (well, maybe more than a little), but all in all, it was a fun time.

On a more serious note, I shall forever be grateful to Ben for his empathy because it was during the winter of this school year that my father passed away and Ben took the reins (not to be confused with his last name) for all of our classes for the week I was absent. He and several of his intern pals even attended my father's funeral, for which I was deeply touched. This "Lord Jeff" (the original Amherst mascot named for Lord Jeffrey Amherst) holds a special place in my heart as someone who reminded me that life requires a bit of fun to be interspersed with the challenges of daily living.

Mike Mangan, Boston College, Chestnut Hill, Massachusetts, 1994–95

Mike Mangan called home Carlisle, Pennsylvania, the location of the United States Army War College. I mention this because Col. Al Shine spent time teaching at the War College following his stint as CMA commandant. Yet someone else came to mind when I thought about Mike. Doogie Howser was a made-for-TV character who worked as a physician when his age belied his competence. That youthful appearance would give pause to anyone seeking medical attention from such a neophyte. Nonetheless, Mike Mangan arrived fully prepared to excel in his intern year, but he did bring with him a youthful countenance that prompted many of us to sit up and take notice.

The first time I met him, I could swear that he looked as if he were twelve years old. I reminded him that he should hold on to that physical attribute for as long as he could. Who cares if he would be carded whenever he ordered alcohol? I suspect he probably did, but it did prompt some good-natured ribbing from both of us.

Mike, like many interns with whom I worked, possessed a strong background in American history, and I entrusted him to take charge for a week during my absence when I was in the United Kingdom. Mike's athletic assignment was made with our swimming and diving programs. He distinguished himself in both high school and college by swimming competitively, and perhaps for the first time in my Culver tenure, I spent some time in our natatorium, observing his coaching talents. It always amazed me to witness an intern whose passion could be transferred to his students and athletes, and this proved just as valid for Mike. His excitement for his sport and diligent work ethic would be mimicked by his star swimmers and divers. Therein encapsulates a motivating factor in the continued support of the faculty intern program. Thank you, Mike Mangan, for maintaining and building upon the strengths of this indispensable program. This was also the first year that Culver hired female faculty interns for the triple-play contributions that they would make along with their male counterparts. It marked another milestone in Culver's progression to equalize male and female roles at the Academies.

Candice Jimerson, Dartmouth College, Hanover, New Hampshire, 1995–96

If ever an intern arrived on the scene to establish her mark upon the entire campus, it undoubtedly fell upon the shoulders of Miss Candice Jimerson. Candice's approach to life rested upon the fact that she would let no stone go unturned in her quest for excellence. The rigor that she demanded of our students was miniscule compared to the demands that she placed upon herself. As a Dartmouth graduate and Gary, Indiana, native, she brought with her a supreme command of her academic discipline in American history as well as finely honed interpersonal relationship skills. As my first female faculty intern, Candice arrived already polished in maturity, rhetoric, and decorum. I honestly can state with unabashed certainty that she needed little to no guidance from me.

The student life office coveted her leadership skills on so many occasions that sometimes I felt as if she was pulled in too many directions that would deter her from expected intern experiences. But Candice never failed. Speaking to the entire student body and often to the Culver Girls Academy, she exemplified the ideals of Culver in promoting responsibility, character, and achievement. The two of us enjoyed a mutually benefiting classroom relationship. I learned much from Candice's no-nonsense yet accommodating individualized approach to classroom management and inducement of student motivation. Unquestionably, she was widely popular with students and her faculty peers. I can still visualize several standing ovations at convocations she received throughout her year with us. Perhaps the most revealing comment that I could make would be that as incoming History Department chair, I offered Candice a position of her own choosing at the conclusion of the school year. I knew of a vacancy, and I was willing to tailor her teaching schedule to accommodate her interests. Alas, regrettably, she turned down my proffer to begin work on her graduate degree at Harvard University. There you have it: I could never compete with "Hahvahd." That crimson and white H shield from Cambridge, Massachusetts, apparently was simply too irresistible for Candice. As disappointed as I was, I could not blame her because countless opportunities on bigger horizons awaited.

Joey Schotland, Amherst College, Amherst, Massachusetts, 1996–97

How does one follow in the footsteps of Miss Jimerson, who achieved legendary status after only one year of the faculty intern program? One turns to Joey Schotland, whom many administrators concluded was the perfect match for Joseph Horvath.

Joey's academic background in Russian area affairs, including both history and government, was enough alone to be worthy of a good pairing with me. What I came to appreciate was that his temperament and outlook on life paralleled mine. It was if the mirror's reflection was merely a younger, better-looking version of me. A native of Washington, DC, and nephew of John Deutsch, former director of the CIA, Joey brought with him both the pedigree and the knowledge of government and politics. Consequently, it made logical sense that Joey would coteach the advanced placement government and politics courses with me. It soon became obvious that I needed to yield to him as the lead instructor in these courses, and I found myself more and more fascinated with his lessons.

I remember thinking about a graduate school professor of mine, Dr. Howard Mowen, who engaged his students with captivating personal accounts of surviving Nazi Germany. In much the same manner as Professor Mowen, Joey held the attention of his students by storied accounts of the nature of the American polity spliced with personal anecdotes from those in the federal government. Joey's star illuminated most brightly when we began the second semester with a course on comparative governments and with a study of Russia's political system.

Together we were able to provide our students with depth and breadth of understanding Russian and Soviet mindsets. Joey's detailed notes for all the classes he taught with me could be laminated for posterity. They were that informative and helpful to both instructor and student alike.

Lest I give the impression that Joey was all cerebral, I make mention that he also served as an assistant coach within our football program. Although I cannot make personal comment upon his coaching abilities, the varsity coach indicated to me on many occasions that Joey's knowledge and techniques of the game were both substantive and motivational to his players. Was it difficult to say goodbye to Joey at the conclusion of the academic year? You bet it was! Again, much like with Candice Jimerson, I enticed Joey to remain with us at Culver, but he was intent at working for the Teach for America program by giving his talents to the inner-city school system of Baltimore. I marveled at his sincere desire to work with students far different from those with whom he engaged at Culver. Following his two-year stint with Baltimore, Joey enrolled and completed his advanced degree in Russian studies at Harvard. That crimson school along the Charles River snagged another one from me!

Bill Freehling, Wake Forest University, Winston-Salem, North Carolina, 1997–98

ACC country and a Baltimore, Maryland, native, brought Bill Freehling to Culver, and this Demon Deacon proved that his transition to the Midwest occurred with no obstacles. Frequently, those interns who did not possess Midwestern roots might struggle with the nature of small-town Americana in the midst of Indiana. Bill slid neatly into his intern responsibilities by drawing little attention to himself. He revealed to all of us that his unassuming demeanor allowed for an instant rapport with students and faculty.

Bill worked with me in several American history classes, one of which was designed for the international students. An integral aspect of that course's curriculum would be to help strengthen the vocabulary of those students for whom English was a second language. Bill's journalism background and command of lexicon proved fortuitously helpful in this regard. Having taught this course for multiple years, I can attest that this is a challenge as much for the instructor as it is for the students. Bill excelled in providing both rigorous and rewarding experiences for these students, and one might imagine that he was wildly popular with CMA and CGA.

Bill's warm-hearted spirit and friendly disposition carried over to the athletic and student life arenas. His work with many of our international students transferred quite nicely to the tennis courts where he coached and displayed his own talents, perhaps not quite at Wimbledon level but proficient, nonetheless. As the school year approached its end, Bill gifted me with a large, framed array of photos of our year spent with one another. I still possess that treasured item, and I think of "Dollar Bill" whenever I gaze upon it on my office wall. His friendship and collegiality were priceless to me in 1997–98, and my memories of him remain indelibly etched as a kind and caring young man.

Ben Croucher, Siena College, Loudonville, New York, 1998–99

I came to appreciate Ben's laid-back approach to all aspects of his life as someone who would not allow challenges to ruffle his feathers. This clearly was someone whom I could learn from as I found difficulty multitasking with my own challenges.

I recollect quite vividly Ben once telling me "Not to sweat the small stuff." My personal issue was that I rarely could differentiate between the "small" and the "large" stuff. On the surface, Ben approached his lessons for his American history and government classes in a seemingly cavalier manner. Perhaps I misjudged him a bit because he was prepared for each day's presentation. I suspect that this may have been an extension of what appeared to be endeavors that did not require much "sweating or perspiration," as he would retort. Eventually, I came to understand that Ben's contributions to both the football and basketball programs as well as the student life demands also revealed his cool, informal, easy-going nature. I did notice a time, however, when Ben's pulse beat more rapidly: NCAA basketball's March Madness and Syracuse University. He was a die-hard fan of the Orange. Many a conversation involved Big East Conference versus Big Ten Conference prowess when it came to the roundball. I think he won most of those debates. Upon close reflection, I don't recall that Ben and I came to know each other as well as we might have. I think that my department chair responsibilities occupied more of my time this year than normal, and as such, this impeded opportunities to spend more time with Ben away from the classroom. I regret that I may have shortchanged him as a mentor.

Will Slade, Carleton College, Northfield, Minnesota, 1999–00

Hailing from Indianapolis and matriculating to Carleton College, Will brought his entrenched Midwest roots with him. Combined with the fact that he was a tennis aficionado and coached both the CMA and CGA tennis teams, we shared similar backgrounds and interests. He played competitively in both high school and college, and his expertise on the tennis courts benefited the young men and women whom he instructed.

Much like the coaching that occurred on the old courts near the horse stables, Will worked diligently to prepare lessons in American government that would stimulate civic responsibility. He brought forth in many discussions the necessity for being informed about the American polity and issues confronting our nation. Politics often gets a bad rap as being corrupt and impractical. Certainly, a case can be made that indeed politics could not be more removed from citizens' lives, but Will provided countless examples of practicality in his lessons. I recall him challenging the students to contemplate a profession in which politics could not play a role. Medicine, business, law, the environment, and so many more rely upon federal and state governments to play roles in the lives of the workers. Will Slade illustrated why this particular course of study would be useful to students long after they departed Culver. I appreciated his farsighted approach in studying about the American polity. Once again, I was blessed to work with an intern who served as an exemplar for his students because of his character, work ethic, and graciousness.

Chris Baudo, Hamilton College, Clinton, New York, 2000–01

A native of Buffalo, New York, and born on the day that we celebrate the birth of Christ, Chris Baudo may very well have exemplified as many Christlike attributes of anyone I have ever met. Well, that may be a stretch since I know a couple priests and nuns. Nevertheless, Chris's profound respect, consideration, and kindness for others were genuine. Noting that Chris was also a hockey jock might appear contradictory to the aforementioned description. After all, many in the hockey world were more inclined to end up in a bench-clearing brawl. After spending a year with Chris, I would have a difficult time envisioning his participation in such a skirmish. From the beginning of the year until its conclusion, Chris referred to me as "sir," and this may well have been the most authentic "sir" of the multitude of salutations I heard on campus. The CMA hockey coaches all concurred that Chris brought forth both expertise and fervor for the sport and welcomed him as an integral component of the hockey staff.

Chris worked closely with me in teaching courses in American government and politics. I observed his growth as a gifted instructor as the year progressed, and I reminded myself how fortunate I was to have him as an intern collaborating with me. In December (and during the height of hockey season), I came to rely upon Chris to absorb classroom teaching duties full-time. Undergoing surgery would necessitate me missing some class time, and Chris not only excelled in my absence but also ventured to my home after each class day concluded and before hockey practice commenced to inquire if I needed any special care. Chris's concern for me during this time underscored just what a considerate fellow he was. I would never forget this, and several years later when one of the Culver hockey coaches saw him (he was then at the Gunnery School in Connecticut) at an Eastern prep school tournament, Chris sent along a message of thanks to me for serving as his mentor during his intern year. His gratefulness toward Culver, the CMA hockey coaches, and me served as a reminder of how fortunate I was to work with such a Christlike gentleman.

Jesse Rice, Furman University, Greenville, South Carolina, 2001–02

Jesse! Jesse! Jesse! How do I begin to characterize the year spent with this Conway, South Carolina, native and Paladin from Furman University? Of all my experiences with interns, I am most disappointed with my own efforts to assist Jesse Rice. Consequently, I must honestly address my own shortcomings in mentoring this young man. Jesse worked with me in American government classes, and perhaps this was not the most appropriate course for which he was prepared. I recognize in hindsight that I could have used our preparation time more for tutorial purposes. I remember a former English Department chair who resorted to tutoring some of his new hires in basic grammar and expository writing so that they could employ those techniques and skills in the classroom. Some of these instructors were grateful, and some resented this tutelage. I believe that Jesse could have benefited greatly with more "coaching" from me. That said, I honestly believe that Jesse's forte existed in the music field. He loved playing his guitar, and in fact, later after his time with us, he was able to record some rather fine country-western music. Jesse, as a very "cool-looking" dude, according to some of his students, built upon that country-boy charm when interacting with the various Culver constituencies. Jesse's love of soccer allowed him to share that passion with CGA soccer. As a footnote, Jesse Rice did indeed find his niche in Nashville. He has recorded numerous country-western albums, and I just so happened to listen to a few of them. Actually, they are quite good, and Jesse is finding success in a field far removed from his intern days on the soccer fields, with barrack life, and in the government classroom at Culver. Good for him!

Mike Hass, College of William & Mary, Williamsburg, Virginia, 2002–03

As a CMA graduate, Mike Hass knew the ins and outs of Culver long before he arrived as an intern, fresh from graduating from the College of William & Mary. Mike distinguished himself as an outstanding scholar-athlete and military leader of CMA, and he brought those talents and achievements with him in his role as a History Department intern. I was not fortunate enough to have instructed Mike during his days as a CMA cadet, but I gratefully accepted the role to serve as his faculty mentor. We labored together in American government classes, and it became most discernible rather quickly that Mike was well-prepared to solo in his own sections of American government. The fact that after his intern year he enrolled in law school illustrated his knowledge and interest in the American polity.

As a native of the area (Mike's home was in nearby Knox), Mike required little adjustment to rural Indiana life. Coupled with the fact that he befriended two former instructors and coaches to whom he gave considerable credit for inspiring him, Mike discovered the Culver intern experience to be a comfortable one. His allegiance to Coach Chastain and the cross-country and track programs allowed him to continue his addiction with running. He and Coach Chastain continued their same relationship that had been forged when Mike ran competitively for CMA. In a similar fashion, Mike and Dr. Jacquie Erwin renewed their mutual fondness and respect for one another. Dr. Erwin's English courses demanded rigorous preparation on the part of both instructor and student, and the two of them became colleagues, sharing with each other the latest vocabulary lists to enhance student lexicons. Both Coach Chastain and Dr. Erwin undertook roles of mentoring Mike that allowed me to learn from both of them. I was grateful that Mike connected and grew from working with all three of us, and we likewise profited enormously from our work with Mike. Collaborative learning at its best!

Asher Rolfe, Wesleyan University, Middletown, Connecticut, 2003–04

The quiet but confident disposition of Asher Rolfe earmarked him for success as a faculty intern. I recognized Asher to be humble yet eager to learn about teaching. He approached his responsibilities with cautious optimism and professionalism. It proved to be most discernible that Asher wanted to utilize this "trial year" as a proving ground for his abilities as a classroom instructor and coach in a boarding school environment. If that appears to be precisely what was intended by the faculty intern program, then Asher would be the prime candidate to serve as its poster boy. In fact, Asher took a position with Norfolk Academy in Virginia following his stint with us at Culver.

The rapport that the two of us developed stretched well beyond the classroom as Asher and I enjoyed similar political orientations, travel pursuits, and reading appetites. Our conversations in all three arenas fostered further discussions and allowed the two of us, in spite of such an age discrepancy, to become fast friends. I know that this particular year was a favorite of mine, and I had to look no further for a reason than the opportunity to work daily with Asher. His knowledge of the American polity revealed strong academic preparation in high school as well as at Wesleyan University. His style of teaching may have been a bit more low-key than mine, but he supremely maintained both rigor and enthusiasm with his lessons. His participation as coach with our wrestling program displayed more assertiveness, but I am certain that this was due primarily to the nature of the sport. Admittedly, I knew little of wrestling techniques, but I appreciated Asher endeavoring to instruct about takedowns and holds. He may even have displayed that wry sense of humor by noting that "wrestlers have all the moves."

Toward the close of the school year, I hosted an extensive family reunion at Culver, and Asher was my guest. I wanted many of my relatives to meet him because he had become part of me, part of my family. Like so many other chapters that would close, this year's ending culminated with a sad goodbye to Asher, my good and dear friend. I was fortunate to meet him once again when he ventured to Indiana with his soon-to-be wife the following year. We were both excited to reconnect with one another, and I took great pride in learning that he was establishing himself in private school life in the Commonwealth of Virginia.

Avery McGlenn, Colgate University, Hamilton, New York, 2004–05

My second female intern, and my first Canadian! Can you sing "O Canada"? I believe that I first heard this song at the start of a hockey game. No great surprise that Avery, hailing from western Canada (Leathbridge, Alberta), brought with her a talent and love for hockey. This time our girls' program was the benefit of someone whose expertise and love of the game could be mimicked by her players. Avery's diminutive stature belied her strength and agility on ice. Clearly, I was no judge of hockey prowess, but I took notice that coaches in both the CMA and CGA programs considered Avery to be instrumental in the development and success of Culver girls hockey.

Avery worked with me in American government and politics courses. Her Canadian background provided a perspective that allowed the students to make comparisons between two systems: parliamentary and presidential. I think it would be a fair assessment to note that Avery grew into her position as classroom instructor. Initially, her soft-spoken nature underscored her inexperience. However, as the year progressed, she became more and more confident in her teaching abilities. Quite normal to acquiring knowledge of a discipline, Avery worked diligently to master the American polity. I was quite grateful for Avery this particular year because, as department chair, I was allowed to work on some particularly challenging issues dealing with both personnel and curriculum. She stepped forward to assume major teaching responsibilities for us. I found it rather prophetic that Avery shared a birthday with Culver's own hockey legendary coach, Al Clark. Somewhere out there in the Colorado Rockies, where she ventured, I suspect that Avery is carving out her own illustrious status.

Johnny Warren, Wabash College, Crawfordsville, Indiana, 2005–06

Johnny, a native of Fort Wayne, Indiana, joined Culver from the all-male Wabash College. As with several other interns, Johnny was a mild-mannered fellow who gradually came out of his shell as the year progressed. He worked with me in American government classes, and his development as an engaging classroom instructor also matured with more experience that he gained from fall to spring. Johnny's strength became evident when social issues of the day were being bantered in seminar discussions. Johnny encouraged his students to examine the roles that national and state governments played in many of these hot-button topics. Focusing an emphasis upon cultural versus political and/ or economic forums allowed the curriculum for government to expand a bit, and I was pleased to witness such new opportunities for teaching and learning.

Johnny may have been one of the few interns who was not inclined toward athletics. His involvement with the Boy Scouts on campus did provide him with opportunities to engage students outside the classroom. I honestly remember little about the Boy Scouts on campus, other than they did meet periodically, usually at Woodcraft Camp. Additionally,

Johnny assisted with the speech team. His background in rhetoric from Wabash proved invaluable to many of the students who competed throughout the winter months. Many of the discussions that Johnny and I shared revolved around literary or cinema classics. His knowledge of the movies far exceeded mine, but I could usually rely upon him to relay what films were worthy of watching. I wish that I had maintained contact with Johnny to help guide me through the Oscars each year. Usually, I am clueless because I have watched none of the nominated films for the major awards. Yet another shortcoming of mine!

Benjamin Au, Carleton College, Northfield, Minnesota, 2006–07

Benjamin, much like Mike Mangan, possessed that youthful look that most assuredly would be an asset to him the more that he aged. Doogie Howser may no longer have dominated the television airwaves, but I still felt his presence, particularly when working with Benjamin. I certainly meant nothing disparaging by this because my own advancing age found that I coveted anyone who could appear younger than what chronology dictated. I suspect that Benjamin's boyish looks gave pause to many of his students who appeared older than he was. As with many situations in life, as we become better acquainted with one another, outward appearances become secondary to what lies within. The mind and heart take precedence, and such was the case for Benjamin with his students in American government class. The students learned to trust their instructor's desire to provide stimulating lessons that could be relevant in their lives. I know that Benjamin exerted countless hours in his preparation, and I applauded him for such an industrious work ethic. Benjamin also assisted with CGA soccer, and this responsibility was one that energized him. He organized practices that mimicked his prepared lessons for American government class. I regret that I did not follow his team as much as I should have. Benjamin and I concluded a very fine year together. I continued to covet his youthful appearance, and he did similarly for my wily, veteran experience. Sometimes the hands of time can be so exasperating!

Jordan Nies, Bucknell University, Lewisburg, Pennsylvania, 2012–13

After the five-year hiatus from mentoring interns, I was overjoyed to welcome Jordan Nies, from Basking Ridge, New Jersey, to the Humanities Department and American government class. I suspect that the interlude between Au and Nies gave me a fresh perspective and enthusiasm for my role as mentor to a recent college grad. Upon reflection, 2012–13 proved to be a most enjoyable year, and Jordan proved to be a primary reason for such a new lilt in my teaching step. Jordan brought a dynamism into his intern duties. He was a lacrosse jock, and he developed a firm commitment to CMA lacrosse as an assistant to Jon Posner, the head coach. Coach Posner wanted to retain Jordan beyond his intern year, and we were able to entice him to remain at Culver for more than one year. I could not have been more supportive because Jordan's professionalism, demeanor, and industriousness carried over from the lacrosse field to the classroom. Bucknell scholastically prepared him well. He possessed a critical thinking mind, and he inculcated that facet of learning into the American government classes which he instructed. I appreciated the fact that he proposed that students think about their widely held views, and oftentimes he encouraged them to challenge those same views, many of which were ones held by family. To be sure, he was vigilant in not ruffling feathers, but he also laid the groundwork for these high school seniors to set their sights for college as springboards for examination and questioning of political, economic, and social norms. Jordan was not flashy, nor was he a flash in the pan. His low-key disposition served him well with the students as they viewed him as someone with whom they could engage without fear of judgment. I too benefited as much as any student because Jordan's infectious eagerness prompted me to respond in kind. For several years, I had missed interacting with recent college graduates and learning from and growing with them. Thanks to Jordan, I was able to capitalize upon our dynamic duo relationship. We had fun, we worked diligently, and usually we were successful. Could we have asked any more of one another?

Adam Spinella, Dickinson College, Carlisle, Pennsylvania, 2014–15

Bow, New Hampshire. Anyone ever hear of that hamlet? I had not, and then entered Adam Spinella, a native of Bow, as the twenty-fifth and final intern in my Culver tenure. Was it just me, or did interns appear to be getting younger and younger with each passing year? No, not another Doggie Howser, but youthful, nonetheless. I concluded that my age had long since caught up with me, after being in the teaching world over forty years.

Adam played basketball. Adam loved basketball. Adam lived basketball. The two of us debated about the game on countless occasions. I would mention Bob Cousy, Oscar Robertson, and Bill Russell. He countered with Steph Curry, LeBron James, and Kevin Durant. Somehow, lost in the middle of these eras, Magic, Bird, and Michael appeared in dialogue. I would agonize over the fact that today's game wasn't really considered basketball, at least as I remembered it. Adam reminded me that I was living in the ancient past; he made it sound as if I lived during the original Greek Olympics and the game had passed me by. We certainly enjoyed our times together, jabbering about the game of roundball.

We enhanced our relationship through discourse about political issues confronting the nation and the world. Adam shared that his mother was a bit more progressive, and his father leaned more to the conservative spectrum. No surprise that I took an immediate liking to his mother when we met. I wondered why I never did meet his father. Perhaps Adam knew better. As a graduate of Dickinson, Adam came to Culver well-versed in our academic discipline of government and politics. I was impressed with his ability to crystalize a lesson for his students. His organizational skills for lesson preparation helped him acquire further depth of understanding of the American polity. As a result, his students had little difficulty grasping the functions of the three branches of government, the roles played by the media, political parties, and interest groups, and the formation of public policy. In essence, Adam and I came to believe that if all Culver graduates comprehended these subsets of government, then they would play vital roles as responsible citizens. Therein lay the purpose for the course. Like Jordan Nies before him, Adam remained at Culver for an additional two years. Although we no longer directly worked with one another, I was overjoyed to see him experience his role within the Admissions Department. Obviously, he continued to help guide CMA basketball to new heights.

The Twenty-Five in Conclusion

To put these young men and women into perspective, I would offer the following: although I came to know some better than others, each of them, in varied and significant ways, impacted me as an instructor and person far more than I could ever have reciprocated. I assure that this is not mere modesty or humility on my part. No one could ever mistake me for possessing those attributes. To those former interns whom I neglected to help negotiate better the twists and turns of living an intern life, I apologize. To all of these twenty-five, I consider myself gratefully blessed that our lives intersected, albeit ever so briefly.

Ye Men of History,
Ye Men of Culver

As chair of the History Department and then Humanities Department, I was privileged to be involved in the hiring, guiding, and promoting of numerous instructors. Some of these folks stayed but a short while; however, several carved paths in teaching at the Academies for an extended time. In doing so, these instructors became both "ye men of history" and "ye men of Culver." The following are the ones who remained as I closed the chapter to my Culver career. I composed this letter in 2016 to affirm my appreciation and support for each of them.

Comrades:

Forgive me this rather unusual manner of parting ways with you, but as I thought of my time with each of you, I could not help but take pride in the fact that I paved a small part in your Culver paths. In each of your cases, I spoke glowingly to the administration of your promise and talents that you brought with you to this hallowed and unique school "behind the corn silk curtain." I am further reminded by the fact that I have learned far more from you than you ever could from me, and I am a better person because of our paths intersecting. Thank you, my good comrades, for all that you have provided to Culver, to your students, and to this humble servant.

Entrance into Culver: 1996

Ed Kelley, I owe you my deepest appreciation as one of my first hires. I vividly recollect Francis Ellert informing me of someone I needed to meet, namely his fellow John Carroll compatriot. Francis and I laboriously got down on our hands and knees, cleaning your apartment so that you would not be inclined to head back to Cleveland once you saw the premises you were assigned. My back still aches from that day of cleaning. I am taken aback by your devotion to your students and this school by promoting the triumphs of our student-athletes and notably outstanding academic achievements in the classroom. I loved the fact that I transitioned from "Uncle Joe" to "Grandpa Joe" when I was invited by your own three children to attend St. Michael's grandparents day in Plymouth. Mary Kate, Tommy, and Maggie will always have a special place in my heart if for no other reason that they are the motivation for you becoming a practicing Roman Catholic again. I am touched by the fact that you have retained the first note that I wrote you as inspirational in your own growth as a teacher. Finally, I am awestruck that you remember each April 29 as the day in which my dear mother passed into God's kingdom. I am respectfully humbled!

Entrance into Culver: 1997

Andy Dorrel, do you recall our first meeting? We were attending an AP conference at St. Mary's College, and you spoke about your time at Crown Point High School. I admittedly coveted your talents and desire to work at an institution whose values mimicked yours. Yes, I actively sought you to fill a vacancy that I knew was pending. This proved to be one of my greatest coups at Culver, and your service in the athletic arena is matched by your growth and success in the field of economics, particularly with assuming the role as AP instructor of micro- and macroeconomics. Your role as a devoted father to Owen, Elliot, and Henry earmarks you as a consummate proactive parent who also has guided and supported so many of your own students and football players. Parents of those students and players have entrusted you with their most precious commodities, namely their sons and daughters. You have grown from errors and mistakes that we all make, and you allow those with whom you interact to do the same. The $64,000 question will be how you handle Owen, Elliot, and Henry's matriculation to that school in Greencastle. Finally, your intentional devotion to words of inspiration from coaches of all sports are words by which we can all live and grow, and you have embraced that message to its fullest. Besides, no one can roof a home better than Dorrel and Company. My own domicile in Michigan was a testament to this. Finally, please know that forever I shall be a supporter of Team Dorrel. I am transitionally moved!

Entrance into Culver: 2001

Richard Battersby, I knew that I was in the midst of scholarship and conviction when I first observed you in the classroom. Your commanding stature, knowledge base, and of course, that British dialect speaking about the American experience distinguish you from the typical American history teacher who frequently spends more time at coaching clinics than he does in preparing lessons. I admire your approach in the classroom like no other I have witnessed in all of my forty-four years of teaching. No one will ever mistake you for mincing words, and I have always appreciated your candor and your insights. Unquestionably, your students have come to regard you as esteemed mentor and master of both subject content and builder of skills. I know that if I ever landed on *Who Wants to Be a Millionaire,* you would be my phone-a-friend. I admire your patience and endurance in dealing with matters for which you have little control. Sometimes committee work is little more than a rubber-stamping of a preordained outcome, yet you conscientiously contributed your insights. Richard, your impact upon the department and the campus at-large will be felt long after your departure. The importance of studying about and learning from history has always remained front and center in your objectives for your courses. There is an adage in life that we all come "full circle," and I suspect that will be the case again as this country comes to terms with a population who has little understanding and appreciation for history. Remember, my friend, history is for all ages—even a history taught by a Brit who confounded his American students. I stand in awe!

Entrance into Culver: 2004

John Buggeln, my first introduction to you came as
somewhat of a surprise in that I was unaware of your
interest in returning to the Midwest from Delaware.
I am not certain that I can recollect if we even had
a vacancy in the department at the moment we met.
However, once we engaged one another, I knew
instantly that your pedigree more than qualified you
as a gentleman and scholar. I distinctly recall my own
entrance into Culver in 1982 when I met numerous
highly qualified historians whom I would categorize as
gentlemen and scholars. In so many significant ways,
you emulated each of those legendary Culver icons
of the not-so-distant past. I came to think of you as
the proverbial Mr. Chips of boarding school fame
because you thrust yourself into arenas that extended
your own gifted teaching. From our Shanghai foreign
language school exchange program to our global
studies expansion, you have broadened the meaning
of learning beyond the far reaches of the classroom
environment. Sailing smoothly with the winds that
traverse Lake Max, I marveled at the energy you
exuded in the drive from Valpo each and every day,
and quite often on weekends. You have remained
positive, helpful, and caring in each of your endeavors
with students and colleagues. It strikes me that you,
perhaps like no other on campus, have reached out
to everyone to demonstrate that cross-disciplinary
studies are integral in cultivating student and teacher
awareness of the connectivity that learning imbues. I
am figuratively and literally transformed.

Entrance into Culver: 2005

Andy Strati, our first conversation occurred where else but in a pub! Little did we know at that arranged meeting that we would have multiple opportunities to engage one another over a variety of libations that numbed our senses but not our minds. Well, OK, maybe our minds too! I knew immediately that your sense of humor was one that I could appreciate and replicate without hesitation. That dry, caustic, infectious, and witty disposition would make us ideal colleagues and travel companions. Barry in York, England, is still waiting for our return because one of us retired to bed far earlier than the other, and I suspect that he is still trying to receive his tip from the one who needed more sleep than drink.

Andy, you are a trusted and admirable fellow. That may appear to be somewhat hollow on the surface, but when one examines the attributes that a friend seeks in another, that is precisely what one desires: trustworthiness and admiration. We have shared our successes and failures. We have shared our joys and sorrows. We have shared our goals and fears. We have shared! Perhaps Laken Alles, the wise lad from your Honor Council, said it best when he suggested that Mr. Strati and Mr. Horvath are quite similar in persona. You may not take this as complimentary, but I assure you, Andy, I regard this remark as one of the most meaningful utterances ever spoken to me. I am richly blessed!

Entrance into Culver: 2006

Gary Christlieb, you arrived on campus with your arm in a sling, and my initial reaction was "Is this part of the wounded warrior crusade? Are we supposed to hire this guy because he is damaged goods?" I learned quickly that you are one of the most accommodating people I have ever encountered. When you offered to assist others, you have done so genuinely with a sincere desire to serve others. This has translated into countless and tireless years of mentoring your students, your basketball players, and many of your colleagues in and out of the department. As department chair, I could rely upon you to be ever vigilant in all of your classroom responsibilities and offer advice and counsel to those who worked with you at the eleventh-grade level. Your introduction into the Civil War course provided an excellent avenue into elective offerings at the senior level that culminated with spring break trips that reinforced the lessons from Gettysburg to Appomattox to intoxicate our students in the field of history. Personally, I am indebted to you for helping me with coverage of my government classes during absences from campus. Most important is that I appreciate your level-headedness and tranquil nature in a world that finds itself embroiled in turmoil on so many occasions.

Finally, I have come to recognize that despite our different allegiances to the Hoosiers and Spartans, we are joined by our unity in celebrating the Big Ten achievements (sans the University of Michigan, of course). I am eternally grateful!

Entrance into Culver: 2008

Kurt Christiansen, perseverance pays dividends, and you embody this attribute as much as anyone I have met. It may have taken two opportunities for the gods of Culver to recognize your merits, but luckily for all of us, the gods did give you a second look. That second glance translated into one of remarkable leadership qualities. Your devotion to improvement in quality instruction cannot be marginalized. It is both gratifying and uplifting to witness your own growth as department chair of the largest entity on campus. I recognize, from personal experience, that the enormity of the task of attending to the needs of such a diverse group of personalities can be overwhelming, and you have met this challenge in a forthright manner. I remind myself that you engaged in rigorous graduate course work in New York and prepared yourself to master a discipline (government and politics) far different from what you had studied, all the while rearing a family of three youngsters. This is something I cannot even begin to fathom attempting to accomplish. Jack, Sarah, and my namesake, Joey, will only have to look to their father for guidance, support, and leadership as they mark time until they too arrive on Culver's doorsteps for matriculation and eventually graduation. I leave in your capably good hands the advanced placement government and politics courses. May you enjoy these students who have a penchant for the world of politics as much as I have had for so many years! I am discernibly impressed!

Entrance into Culver: 2010

J. D. Uebler, you and your lovely wife, Emily, have made the final few years for me at Culver so pleasantly meaningful. The gratification emanates not merely from Emily's delectable treats and meals that she has so graciously prepared for the department but from the mere fact that the two of you are such likable personalities who seek the best in others. J. D., I particularly benefited from working collaboratively with you this past year in American government class. Although you believed that your contributions to the discussions were minimal, they were nonetheless quite illuminating. I always have profited from team-teaching (probably one of the reasons that I have supported the intern program with enthusiasm), in large regard, to being able to learn from colleagues. The newness of teaching each day's lesson brings with it the challenges and joys of working with students. You embrace this approach to tailoring your instruction to each student's level of expertise, ability, and potential. Clearly, you have rejected painting the canvas with the stroke of a broad brush, and rightly so! I have witnessed your own growth in leadership in your role as curricular chair of the department. Through many conversations, both passionate and important, you continue to spur teachers to think cognitively about what they do and why they do it. I would be remiss if I did not mention that your life has taken on an added joy with the addition of Miss Eva! I may not be present for the countless awards and distinctions that she will accrue as a CGA student, but rest assured I know that her parents will be there every step of the way to support, guide, and love her. I am delightfully amazed!

Ye Men of Culver

Ye men of Culver glad praises sing
to God the Father, all glory bring.
He who has brought us safe through the year
May He through life's labors ever be near.
Heroes of Culver leading us on
With glorious honor in battle won.
Lord, may we carry their guidon true
Through age never ending, with valor new. (Culver Academies)

Neighbors, Colleagues, Friends, and Family

I commence this chapter as I severed my working relationship with Culver in 2016. In the process of saying goodbye to the school and home I loved, I was obliged to do the same with the Chastains, my compatriots for over thirty years. This is the letter that I penned for them when we embraced one final time as neighbors, colleagues, friends, and family. Akin to a film that examines characters backward in time, I thought this an appropriate way to describe the abiding relationship that I cultivated with these most special people.

May 2016

To Michael and Anne,

> After thirty-plus years, how does one say goodbye? We have been neighbors, colleagues, friends, and family, and all those relationships have intermingled with one another to create a love that transcends each and every relationship. Allow me this opportunity to reflect upon our time together. I perceptively recall moving into the duplex apartment next to you on November 1, 1985.

Mike, you offered to help me with hauling boxes from the garage into the apartment, and afterward, I think that I offered you a glass of wine. I remember your facial reaction and polite yet puzzled look. You probably thought a budding alcoholic was moving in next door because it was still morning and all I had to offer was some wine. Little did you know that I had more "whine" in me than actual wine.

I remember Jordan, not yet a year old, climbing up the carpeted stairway, thinking how cute he was. Now we reflect upon him and his wife watching their own little boy climbing stairs. I remember Dean Nagy smiling broadly when he saw me pedal Jordan on my bicycle in and around campus. I laughed uproariously at the umbrage that my AP US history students took when Professor Jordan put them to shame by knowing the states and their capitals better than they did. I fondly recall Ashley and Jordan hunting for Easter eggs on a gorgeous spring morning, decked out with their Easter finery. How could I ever forget the "Thanksgiving turkey" that Patrick McHugh prepared for all of us in May? Somehow the turkeys that we used to receive at the holidays stayed frozen and preserved nearly six months later. The memories of Gene Twardosz, humoring us in amusing conversation, are firmly etched in my mind. I know that you, Michael, will never find another track official (and in particular a high jump one) who could be more enthralled and devoted to his duty than I was. I regret now that I was too deliberate and extended the event far longer than needed.

I shall ever be grateful for the heartfelt gifts you bestowed upon me at Christmas and my birthday as well as including me many times over for dinner and picnics (still waiting for that potato salad recipe, Anne, that I guess was never meant to be). We grew together and bonded as we aged and watched our parents do likewise, only eventually to leave us alone on this earth.

I remain in awe of you, Michael, for the devotion and care that you showed your students and athletes over the many years. They came to look to you for guidance and support, and you never turned any away. In many regards, they have come to think of you as their surrogate father.

Anne, you have always been so supportive of Michael in his cross-country and track endeavors, and I know that Michael has always appreciated your willingness to assist him in his devotion to these sports. You have a wonderful marital relationship with one another, and it extends far beyond Michael earning the money and you, Anne, spending it.

Michael, I love you for the mere fact that you have tolerated a neurotic and sometimes emotional cripple next door. Your listening ear and unswerving nature not to be too critical or judgmental of me was far more than I deserved. King Moore referred to me as someone who was not good at beginnings or endings but damn good in the middle. Hopefully, this accounts for something to you as I spent so many of my middling years next door to you. I thank you for the countless walks that we three took, particularly at the conclusion of each school year. That routine was a fitting way to mark the passage of time—the passage of days, weeks, months, and eventually years. I am reminded of my favorite biblical passage (Ecclesiastes 4:9–10). When you get a chance, reread it, and I think that you will both understand its applicability in this case.

As I mentioned, I am not good at goodbyes or endings. So all you need to know is that I am that same neurotic and sometimes emotional cripple that I have always been. May your new neighbor be less abnormal.

The time has come that I must say goodbye to you. Europeans have a much better way of parting company. *Auf Wiedersehen,, au revoir, arrivederci, hasta luego,* and *do svidaniya* all connotate "seeing you again." I prefer their approach of bidding adieu.

In many tangible ways, I wish I did not have to close this chapter because it represents the best part of who I have been. I offer you my love, dear friends, always and forever.

Goodbye.

Mike and I at my final Culver graduation

If the above letter conveys a deep sense of love and appreciation for Michael and Anne Chastain, then it succeeded in what it was intended to accomplish. As my farewell letter indicated, I met the Chastains when I moved next door to them at the 173 North Terrace duplex that we occupied with one another in 1985. For more than thirty years we shared in each other's lives, and we became far more than mere residents sharing the same Academy rental. I suggest that the letter provides ample evidence of the fondness that yielded to love for these dear people. The following will attempt to portray with greater objectivity and clarity their contributions to the greater Culver community.

Anne Marie Pare, born in New England and the daughter of a foreign language instructor, has spent all but a few months of her life in Culver. In fact, one would be accurate in recording that she has resided on North Terrace Drive longer than anyone ever has. Her parents, Al and Penny Pare, moved to Culver and settled around the circle from 173 North Terrace. She experienced both the "town and gown" atmosphere as a Culver daughter. Consequently, her roots have been firmly planted in both community and academy life, and her love for both distinguishes her as uniquely suited to patronize both "town and gown." From serving as an academy switchboard operator to volunteering as a local precinct voting official, Anne has carved out her own niche within Culver society. As a mother to Ashley and Jordan, she was instrumental in the formation of their education, first at Culver Elementary, followed at St. Anne's School in Monterrey, and finally at the Academy. In each case, Anne actively volunteered and supported the schools that fostered a learning and growing environment for her children. Both Ashley and Jordan have distinguished themselves in their chosen fields (Ashley as a researcher of infectious diseases and Jordan as a lawyer), and Anne, as much as anyone, deserves accolades for the patience, encouragement, and love she provided in helping her children become the vibrant, talented, contributing adults that they are.

Michael Elmo Chastain, born in North Carolina, was raised in the southern Indiana town of Mitchell, the hometown of NASA's notable astronaut Virgil "Gus" Grissom. The eldest of four children and with deep farming roots, Michael maintained his Hoosier twang as part of his dialect, even though having lived in Culver for most of his adult life. After graduating from Indiana University in Bloomington, he was hired as a physical education instructor and coach at the Academies in 1974. Nearly fifty years later, he distinguished himself as one of Culver's legends in the truest sense of that achievement.

In reference to historical greatness, Dean Nagy would ofttimes proclaim, "Back when boys were men and men were giants." Such is the case with Michael. Never in the annals of Culver history will there be a greater giant than Coach Michael E. Chastain. I can attest to this acclamation because I repeatedly witnessed this from countless student-athletes who were afforded the privilege of working with their most respected and trusted mentor. One easily could be impressed by the number of cross-country and track athletes who have garnered fame by winning state championships.

Undoubtedly, Michael's coaching abilities and his motivational approach to running have inspired Culver students regardless of their talents and potential. Therein is the key to Coach Chastain's enduring legacy: he never quit on any of his student-athletes, and they never forgot that lesson in life. I learned from some of the runners in my classes that cross-country and track athletes possess a unique psyche; namely, their fragility rises and falls with each successive competition. Somehow, Michael has been able to minimize many of their roller-coaster highs and lows by instilling a calmness amid their adrenaline pumping performances. Many of these attributes one would find within some in the coaching ranks. What distinguished Michael from so many of his peers throughout his career is that he has served in more significant roles than merely coaching cross-country and track. His guidance, support, counsel, and advocacy for each of his proteges were unconditionally provided and gratefully received by each of those students and each of those athletes. Just as significant to the contributions that he has made to the cross-country and track programs are the strides that he led in curriculum reform within the Health Department, Physical Education Department, and Wellness Department. He initiated courses that prepared students for making healthy choices in their own lives, and his infectious leadership in this regard propelled his department colleagues to do likewise. In many ways, he embodied the Greek model citizen of a "healthy body, healthy mind, and healthy soul" better than anyone I have ever encountered.

Michael's humility, compassion, and spirituality are woven together as a fabric of his very being. If this appears to be too grandiose of an assessment of this man, I assure that, if anything, I am minimizing the magnitude of his attributes. He literally has surrendered himself to others in service, in support, and in sacrifice. From his mentoring within the Fellowship of Christian Athletes group to his organization of campus Red Cross blood drives, preparation and organization for arguably the largest yearly contingent of campus visitors at Culver Cross-Country Invitationals, his leadership within the state of Indiana Cross-Country and Track Coaches Association, and his diligent approach to every assignment given to him by the Academies, Michael's diligence and excellence are unsurpassed.

Unquestionably, the history of the Culver Academies could not be recorded without the inclusion of legendary figures. Michael E. Chastain is not only one of those key figures, but when one investigates the totality of his contributions to the life of the institution, it would be difficult to dispute that anyone impacted the school and its constituent groups more than he did. I would be less than candid if I revealed that Michael's esteemed imprints are discernible to all on campus because his presence largely was felt behind the scenes and without considerable fanfare. Nevertheless, for posterity's sake, let me assume the honored distinction of revealing to one and all that I was blessed to witness such a remarkable man: my neighbor, my colleague, my friend, and my family.

Saving the Best for Last
and Closing the Circle

A Final Year before Exiting

My final year of teaching at the Culver Academies was 2015–16, and the summer leading up to that time was ambivalent for me. I did not know how to prepare for ending thirty-four years along the shores of Lake Max. Over half of my life had been spent at this august institution of learning. Two of my closest associates (my teaching comrade, Harry Frick, and my fitness workout partner, Brett Rankert) departed in June 2015, and most of the colleagues who graced this school when I arrived were long deceased or had also retired away from Culver. I knew that the time was ripe (perhaps long overdue in some respects) that I too would take leave.

Seemingly my entire life from age five until age sixty-five had been spent in the world of education (grammar school, junior and senior high school, college undergraduate and graduate, public school teacher in Michigan, and finally at Culver, the private boarding school that I came to call home). How does one really know that one is ready for a new fork in the road? Life's journeys take on many crisscrossing paths, and I certainly was blessed in 1982 to have made the trek from Michigan to

Culver. However, now my sojourn would eventually lead me away from the sights and sounds of which I grew so accustomed. I recall walking the campus many times over, trying to resurrect what once was and what now is. The year 1982 was difficult, a year of transition in my life. As earnest as my efforts were, I simply did not feel as if I belonged or fit in with what I witnessed from my teaching colleagues. Public school teaching could not replicate what I was to experience in the next three-plus decades of my life. Over time and without much contemplative thought, I did find myself becoming the proverbial "Culver man." I wish that words could convey precisely what this entails, but regrettably, I can only equate this with an abiding esteem and affection that one develops for others. Culver with its lake shoreline, adorning spires and gargoyles, statues and monuments, athletic fields, and buildings teeming in history personified life beyond the "corn silk curtain," as the once illustrious Dean Nagy referenced. I repeatedly heard that Culver was the best kept secret in the rural Midwest. Indeed, it has been for all who never traversed its walkways. However, I did amble those concrete sidewalks and dirt-laden paths, and as I so frequently did, I envisioned the faces of so many who walked in these footsteps before and with me. These teachers, interns, counselors, coaches, parents, alumni, and especially students were vividly etched in my thoughts. So many of these Culver men and women I came to know. So many of them I came to appreciate. So many of them I came to respect. So many of them I came to love. It was with this mindset that I embarked upon my final year.

Attention to Classroom Instruction

I knew cerebrally and viscerally that my time rapidly was approaching to hang up the chalk and eraser. That phrase alone would signal that it was perhaps well past time. I cannot even recall the last time that I employed chalk and eraser in the classroom. I reminded myself what a noble profession I had chosen. My father would speak so frequently of his "schoolteacher" son. Since I was the only one of seven siblings in my family who graduated college, I think that both of my parents were enormously proud of this accomplishment. At least this is what I repeatedly told myself because I could never be mistaken for "Mr. Goodwrench". My mechanical aptitude would score negatively on any scale devised by humankind.

I intentionally decided that this year would be markedly different from the previous years in that all my focus would be upon classroom teaching. I literally avoided all Academy directives to educational, pedagogical, and curricular reforms. Without becoming overly critical what Culver had become in its quest to improve itself, I recognized that I was marching to a different drumbeat. Instead, I established a goal for myself to be the best that I could be in the classroom setting. For me this entailed rigorous academic challenges, mastery of subject matter, critical thinking and analysis, and polished communication skills. Everything else became secondary, perhaps even superfluous, to what I deemed essential to scholarship. I spent more time in preparation for lessons that would stimulate, challenge, excite, and oftentimes frustrate the students and me. Equally important, I began to look forward to the newness of each day's lessons. I wanted to be at my best because that is what so many of my own teachers were for me. They gave me their best, and I wanted to replicate their passion and commitment. So many students over the years gave me their best, and I thought that I might have shortchanged them because in my heart of hearts I don't think I had given my all to them. This year would be different. I did not fully comprehend just how different it was to become.

My Mormon Inspiration

Once in a lifetime (or maybe twice) we are blessed to encounter someone who impacts our lives in ways perceived unfathomable. Such was the case with one of my advanced placement government and politics students. I knew from the first day of classes that this young man possessed qualities that I coveted for most of my life. Laken Alles grew up in Utah, but his family had moved to Saudi Arabia several years earlier when he entered

Culver as a repeat sophomore. His father had taken a job with Aramco, and because of that move, the family of seven (parents and five children) experienced living and traveling internationally that certainly broadened Laken's cosmopolitan views.

If ever a teacher could describe his ideal student, I could not find a more apt qualifier than this Mormon lad. In fact, as the year unfolded, I would further my testament of Laken as the ideal son or grandson (in my case). Not a single day throughout the entire academic year elapsed without Laken greeting me with an infectious smile, hearty shake of the hand, and wide-eyed eagerness to learn. Quite early in the year, Laken and I met regularly to discuss spiritual matters, and he appeared excited and passionate to share his devotion to the Church of Jesus Christ of Latter-day Saints. He introduced me to Mormon missionaries living in the Culver vicinity, and I came to realize how committed Laken and these young elders of the church were. Their zeal to spread the messages from the Book of Mormon was both laudable and inspirational.

Having been raised in the Roman Catholic tradition, I was a bit confounded by some of the lessons that Laken and the elders related to me. However, I sought for commonalities that would allow all of us to grow in fellowship with one another. As Advent approached, I gave Laken a Catholic book of Advent and Christmas prayers, and he dutifully read, digested, and reflected upon this as an ecumenical learning opportunity. Before he departed for our Christmas holiday break, Laken gave me a heartfelt note of appreciation for the rapport, support, and love that the two of us developed for one another. Accompanying that letter, he gifted me with a replica pin of a Mormon temple that I proudly wore each day for the remainder of the school year. Each morning that I placed that pin on my shirt or sweater, I thought and prayed for this young man who had given so much more to me than I could ever had bestowed upon him.

Laken shared with me that a temple is a place where one can experience the Lord in a most profound manner, and in the process, one becomes closer to our Savior. Certainly, I have encountered many spiritual young men and women in my years of teaching, but I doubt that I ever came face-to-face with someone who lived each day of the week as he lived on the Sabbath. One lunch conversation at semester break allowed the two of us to take stock of where our lives had evolved since late August. Laken related that he was preparing for his own two-year mission upon graduating from Culver. His words were quite revealing, and a bit unsettling. He soberly stated that he would be anxious to halt the *me* concentration that Culver prepared its students to embrace and begin living a life full of focusing upon *others*. The revelation of this statement focused upon the truth that Culver endeavors to help students develop themselves academically, physically, and spiritually. The disquieting aspect of this proclamation is that I recognized that my protégé would indeed be leaving me in a few months, and I tried to obliterate this thought as this would be something I would have to deal with down the road. The proverbial lesson that all of us experience in letting go of someone we cherish is one of life's most difficult truisms. Once again, my good priest's wise counsel hit home. I remember how much my stomach hurt when we parted from that luncheon conversation.

The usual Midwest winter weather brought with it the usual illnesses that permeate our campus. With one innocent sneeze comes the onslaught of influenza and pneumonia. Seemingly dozens upon dozens of students and faculty would suffer through nagging coughs, headaches, fever, sore throats, runny noses, and the like. Such was the case for Laken.

In late January before the advanced placement government and politics class embarked to observe the Iowa caucuses, both the flu and pneumonia struck Laken. He weathered the trek to Iowa, but upon the return to Culver, his energy level sagged to the depths of the walking dead. With medical assistance from the health center, Laken did rebound a bit, just in time for the winter weekend leave when he spoke to his Mormon congregation about redemption. His mother and eldest sister journeyed from Saudi Arabia to hear the passionate words that Laken spoke. What a loving tribute this family imbues to one another! After the weekend storm that pummeled the area, Laken's mother and sister departed for the return trip to Saudi.

Within a matter of days, Laken's pneumonia resurrected itself, and he was one sick lad. The health center confined him to an isolation room, and each day that I visited him, he appeared sicklier than the day before. My heart went out to him because he struggled with such a persistent cough that weakened his entire immune system. Perhaps my heart ached for his mother even more since she was half a world away, consumed with worry about her precious firstborn. Through God's benevolent graces, Laken eventually made it to spring break and a family excursion to the Turkish isles. Before he joined his family, he experienced his final interview for his mission and was ordained into the Melchizedek Priesthood of the Church of Latter-day Saints. I attended this ceremony, and although I may not have gleaned all of the nuances of this event, I could not have been prouder of him for the devotion he bestowed upon Jesus Christ, his church, his upcoming mission, and his family and friends. I reminded myself once again what a blessing I have received by having my life intersect with this remarkable young man. I recall thinking that the thousands of lives that he will touch in the coming two-year mission will be blessed as well.

My belief in Laken was reinforced the day we arrived back to Culver from our spring break. He emailed me that he was in Chicago, arriving from a flight from Turkey, and asked if I wanted to be included when he opened his letter from the Mormon Church in which he would learn about his assignment for the upcoming two-year mission. Unhesitatingly, I responded, "Of course."

He wrote that this would be the longest and last bus ride that he would take from Chicago to Culver since his anxiety level reached an all-time high, wondering precisely where he would land for the next two years. I received a rap at my back door at 5:00 p.m., and outside stood Laken, his sister, Allie, and his good friend, Lizzie. With the envelope firmly clasped in his hand, Laken readied himself for the destination that was assigned to him. His sister, Allie, called home to Saudi Arabia to have his entire family awakened (it was well after midnight there) so that they could participate in this transformative event. The excitement amid the apprehension gripped all of us from my living room to Laken's home in Dhahran, Saudi Arabia.

As Laken nervously fidgeted with the bulky packet, and Allie held her smartphone for Mom and Dad to observe, I watched with anticipation a loving family, separated by thousands of miles, bond with one another in a way that was reminiscent of a Christmas morning and opening the surprises from Santa. Even Laken's three siblings back in Saudi awoke to celebrate this milestone. When Laken began to read to all of us in my living room and his family in Saudi, tears welled in his eyes, and his voice quivered. I could not have been more supportive of him because he worked so diligently to get to this point in his life.

When he announced that he was assigned to Seoul, South Korea, a moment of silence crept over all of us. I had hoped that he would get to experience an international location because so many of his global experiences would prepare him well to spend his mission abroad. How prophetic this assignment turned out to be the one that his own father received many years before. Now the son would be following in his own father's and our Heavenly Father's footsteps.

After hugs from near and afar, we celebrated this call to serve by having dinner at a local restaurant. I reflected and prayed upon the workings of our Lord. A few weeks earlier, Laken lay in a hospital bed, weak and exhausted from pneumonia, and now, fully recovered, he received the ultimate blessings from his Church of Jesus Christ of Latter-day Saints. Since we were into the Easter season, I contemplated about how a Friday, the day of the crucifixion of our Lord, eventually became a Sunday, the day of His resurrection. Could a better analogy exist?

During parents' weekend at Culver in late April, Laken's dad surprised him with a visit from Saudi Arabia. His father, Tim, stayed with me, and I don't believe that I have ever enjoyed a more delightful parents visit. His love for his son and entire family could not be more evident by the fact that he traveled such a great distance for such a short period of time. However, in that brief weekend encounter, I came to know a man whom I would respect and admire greatly. Tim's warmth and witty disposition underscored what a gift I have received from so many of Culver's parents over the many years that I have engaged them during a special fall or spring weekend. I appreciated his insights and questions that he posed the advanced placement government students when he visited the classroom.

We spent the entire weekend with Laken and his sister, Allie, a sophomore at Culver. Highlights included a visit to Notre Dame and the grotto (the Basilica of Sacred Heart was closed due to several weddings) and numerous dining experiences in and around the area, most notably a Korean restaurant in which Tim and the waitress conversed in fluent Korean. I was impressed, to say the least.

We also observed honor organization presentations, parade with all the Culver trappings, a rugby competition, and of course, a Mormon service at the Plymouth Branch. Perhaps it was at this service that I knew instantly that I liked Laken's father more than I had anticipated I would. Tim provided a testimony to the congregation that he was grateful for the love, care, and devotion that the church had bestowed upon his son and daughter while they were away from him and the rest of the family during the school year at Culver. The tears in his eyes replicated the tears that his son shed a month earlier when he opened his mission assignment letter to South Korea. I too had to wipe away the moist drops that began to stream down my cheeks because I knew that this was the loving bond between a father and his children that can never be broken, no matter how distant the separation or length of time apart.

When it was time to say goodbye to Tim before he departed to Chicago for his return to Saudi Arabia, we embraced one another, and I whispered to him, "God be with you 'til we meet again," words borrowed from a song that I sang with Laken at my first Mormon service. I was truly sad to watch him leave. It was as if I were saying goodbye to a long-lost friend, yet I knew him for only three short days. I reminded myself that Laken is truly blessed to have such a loving, supportive father and mother. I took solace in that fact. I also reminded myself of the countless parents of students over many years at Culver whom I came to respect and admire, just as I had done with Tim during my final parents' weekend at Culver.

Laken and I spent the remainder of the year engaged in conversation about religion, government and politics, family, and service. I attended several more Mormon services, including a major conference at the South Bend Stake in which leaders of the church gave testimony into their belief that Jesus Christ is their personal Savior. Along this path, I met several more Mormon missionaries who, like Laken, were deeply committed to this covenant in their lives. In some ways each of these young men replicated the goodness that I found in my protégé, Laken. Hymn number 152 kept turning over in my mind until the organist commenced with the song. Laken, standing next to me, sang reverently "God Be with You 'til We Meet Again." I knew that these were going to be my farewell words to "my Mormon inspiration" when we would part at graduation.

The final months gave way to weeks, which gave way to days. Numerous people on campus inquired if I had been counting down the days until I closed my Culver way of life. I responded to each one that I had not chosen to do this for fear of allowing this countdown to dominate my existence. I simply wanted to enjoy and revel in each day and each hour with my students. I chose to focus intentionally upon each student individually more than I had done in previous times. At least I told myself that was what I was doing. Maybe I was merely attempting to deflect attention away from me and the feelings of nostalgia that might take center stage. I did everything possible to camouflage my "marshmallow" image.

Laken and I, in Assisi, Italy

Maybe It Really Was Not the Best after All

Perhaps old age really has firmly gripped this body and soul of mine. Many a day in the classroom seemed to linger far longer than I had hoped, and I began to contemplate if I had remained at Culver far too long for effective teaching and learning. However, aside from the physical aches and pains due to aging, my emotions took center stage. I reminded myself, as I had done so often before, that the ancient Greeks believed that a healthy body, a healthy mind, and healthy soul were necessary for balance in one's life.

I prepared a speech for the commencement convocation at graduation weekend in late May. I envisioned this as a gift to all of the students with whom I interacted for the past thirty-four years, even though the vast majority of them would never hear the heartfelt words being penned for them. I wrote and then rewrote and recollected what a colleague had told me about writing. He emphatically instructed that good writing simply does not exist; good rewriting does. No truer words could ever be spoken. Perhaps I never worked so diligently on a written piece as I did this one, in large part because it would be my farewell to Culver.

I am not altogether certain how significant my words were to the audience, but I was grateful for the opportunity to share them with colleagues, friends, and especially students. My final exit was putting Culver in the rearview mirror. Reflections that were once so distinct and transparent soon faded and blurred to obscurity. As we age, life on earth does that sometimes.

I reminded myself that it is important to leave on a high note. So as a postmortem, I suspect that my final year was not all that dissimilar from the previous thirty-three at Culver. I was not as good as I had hoped I would be, and therein completes the never-ending circle of life: aspiring to be better, recognizing that this is not always readily achievable, and going forward to a new day, a new time, and a new beginning. Circles are like that, aren't they?

Epilogue

Boarding school life embodies an existence all to itself. Instructors who extend themselves to students, fellow colleagues, parents in absentia, alumni, administrators, and boards of trustees discover that the visceral complements the cerebral components of their chosen profession. The quest for intellectual curiosity paves the way for success in physics, in French, in calculus, or in history. Student progress in such disciplines indicates that the learning process, delicately woven between dynamic instructors and dedicated students, creates the fabric by which academic success is measured. Much of this achievement is calculable, perhaps even quantitative.

If the preceding chapters validate anything, they authenticate that sheer emotion plays an integral role in boarding school life. Those who rely upon intellect alone are left with little more than a mere faded snapshot of teaching. Those who combine stimulating the intellect with compassion, empathy, humor, and humility discover the poignancy of a featured film. I hope that boarding school instructors throughout this world, peering through their own rearview mirrors, observe epic movies of lives they indisputably impacted and of those who heartfully affected them.

Printed in the United States
by Baker & Taylor Publisher Services